FINDING MY PLACE:

ONE MAN'S JOURNEY
FROM CLEVELAND TO BOSTON
AND BEYOND

By

JUDAH LEBLANG

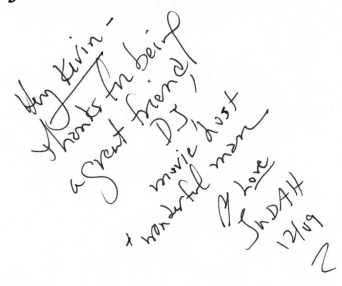

Finding My Place:
One Man's Journey from Cleveland to Boston and Beyond

Published by
Lake Effect Press
21 Bradlee Road #42
Medford, MA 02155
www.lakeeffectpress.com

Author—Judah Leblang
Editor—Anne Brudevold
Technical & Creative Editor—Evan Dana
Cover Design—Peter Sawchuk

www.judahleblang.com
http://judahism.blogspot.com

Publishing Acknowledgments

Versions of some essays in "Finding My Place" have been published or broadcast previously, as listed below:

"The History of My Names," published in the Somerville Journal newspaper; broadcast on WYSO radio, NPR for Dayton, Ohio

"The Other Side," published in Northern Ohio Live magazine

"Papa's Place," published in Northern Ohio Live, broadcast nationally on "The Health Show," produced by WAMC radio, NPR for Albany, NY. Also broadcast on WSKU radio, NPR for Northeast Ohio, WYSO radio

"Life in the Slow Lane," published in the Somerville Journal

"The Road Not Taken," published in Northern Ohio Live

"Everything is Relative," broadcast on "The Health Show" and WKSU radio

"Necessary Losses," published in Bay Windows newspaper, and broadcast on "The Health Show"

"The Price of Silence," published in Bay Windows

"My Training Bra," published in Bay Windows; broadcast on "The Quest of Life," WRPI radio, Troy, NY

Author's Note

This book is a work of creative non-fiction. The vignettes and essays that follow are essentially true; the key events are described as I recall them, subject to the vagaries of my memory. As a young gay boy and an aspiring writer, I observed and noticed the people and places around me in great detail, which I have recreated here.

I have, however, changed the names of some individuals and fleshed out some scenes for dramatic effect. My intention, particularly in Part One, is to convey a sense of the rich world I come from—a Midwestern Jewish world that was both specific and universal. Throughout the collection, my aim is to convey the emotional truth of the place and the people who formed me, along with the place I inhabit today, one largely of my own creation.

TABLE OF CONTENTS

"CLEVELAND IS A PLUM/1981"

So much remains to be written
of a city doused in ash;
the gates of shuttered steel mills and empty docks
echo in eerie silence.

Purgatory on a cold gray lake
fed by a flammable river,
slicing winds and knee-deep snows
embrace the locals like a lover.

Anything was possible here
so my parents said—
A 1940s boom-boom midwestern town,
brewing beer and smelting steel,
a mecca for the working man.

In '48 the Indians won the World Series.
Truman beat Dewey
and Cleveland could do no wrong.
Sixth largest city, anything was possible here.

Then came the riots, dreams delayed too long.
Progressive Cleveland standing still,
ethnic feuds among the clans,
free flowing fear led Whites to a promised land
outside the city limits.

Our first Black mayor came and went,
beaten by the system, and I was born in the suburbs
of this once great city that smelled of smoking wood
and broken dreams and a lake called dead.

Cleveland has the football Browns and the baseball Tribe.
Blacks and Whites mix freely at the games,
driven by that hunger to be the best—
but we never are.

The Indians lose most every game most every year,
and I love them more fiercely for that.
I sit on splintered wood and cheer them on
as fans grow sparse and fall winds come
to our city cold on its stagnant lake.

The Cleveland Press was my newspaper, my daily route.
I ate the sports pages before dinner.
Now the printing presses are still—forever.

The Plain Dealer is left alone—
a plain paper for a shrinking city.
"Cleveland is a Plum" the PD crows,
or dried like a prune, I think.

Anything was possible here,
so my parents said.
And why was it my fate
to watch the rotting of those dreams
echo in eerie silence?

THE PLACE I COME FROM

PART ONE

Dad, Mom, Me (left) and Doug, 1962

BORN TOO LATE

I grew up east of Cleveland in the 1960s and '70s in a suburb called Beachwood. A small, mostly Jewish town located miles from any body of water, the city was originally named for its many beech trees—which were gone by the time we arrived. At some point, when the town was just a village, Beech became Beach.

My father, a city boy lusting for fresh air, often talked about wanting to live further out of the city, surrounded by grass and trees. My mother wanted more space—our house felt cramped, confining for a family of four—soon to be five when my younger brother, Alex, unexpectedly arrived on the scene. Unwittingly, I became the driving force for our move from middle-class University Heights to the more wooded area my father craved after I was in a serious car accident. A year later in 1963, just before I began first grade, we moved into a new four-bedroom colonial in Beachwood, on a quiet street recently carved out of the Northeastern Ohio woods.

At first, our new house and the neighborhood around it seemed magical. We had a comfortable family room with a full-sized, 24-inch Zenith color television. I had my own bedroom—I no longer had to share one with my big brother Doug—with rust-colored carpeting, an extra bed just for guests, and my own faux-mahogany desk and matching bookshelves. In the kitchen, white Formica countertops gleamed, and so did my mother's white tile floor, kept spotless by Donna, our cleaning lady, who took the bus up from the city, five days a week. Our street featured half-empty lots full of tree stumps and shells of new houses, perfect for tree climbing and games of hide-and-go-seek.

My father got a half-acre lot with a few saplings, my mother got her modern house, and I got a chance to walk to school without dodging traffic, sparing Mom's already brittle nerves. It took me a while to figure out that Beachwood was not nirvana, but simply an extension of what I'd already had one town west. True, we lived in a bigger house, and there were more of 'us'—Jews—than 'them'—Christians, particularly the ones my father would talk about in a disgusted voice—the ignorant ones who hated Jews. Eventually, the street filled up with other colonials and split-levels, full of families like ours—business-owners like my Dad, lawyers and doctors, men who had made it on the backs of their immigrant parents.

But even among the Jewish boys who filled my classes, I carried a fundamental sense of difference. Doug was a natural athlete, who played baseball and basketball with the neighborhood boys. Five years younger, I couldn't compete with him, or even hold my own with kids my age. Catching or throwing a baseball was a Herculean task, ("You throw like a girl" was a taunt that followed me into high school.) I channeled my energy into my classes—earning mostly A's and B's, competing with the jocks on our Iowa Basic achievement tests and spelling bees—while I wished I could impress them on the baseball diamond or —better yet—on the wrestling mat.

And so I became a fan, an observer, rooting for those strong men on those Cleveland teams to do what I could not—snag a fly ball, catch a spiral, hit a jump-shot. Those teams, and the drama of professional sports, led me to the city where my father worked as an electrical engineer, and my mother's father, Papa Ben, dispensed his medications at his drug store. My father had season's tickets for the Browns games, and by the age of seven I was sitting with him, cheering along with 80,000 other football fans in Lakefront Stadium, the wind whipping in off the lake, chilled and thrilled by the energy of those fans and the heroic men on the field.

By the time I understood things like divisional playoffs and conference championships, the Browns had faded from great to good. Meanwhile, the Indians were the league doormats, never finishing above third place, and frequently losing far more than they won. How could I not love them, with their futile quest to be the best, to compete, even if every year the result was the same? At 12 or 13, I started to go to baseball games with my friends, riding the ironically-named Shaker Rapid. The rickety yellow cars deposited us downtown, shaken and stirred, where we'd walk half a mile to the stadium, the ushers dozing in the summer heat.

I'd heard stories of 20 or 25 years before, of the Indians' 1948 World Series championship. Like most good things in Cleveland, I was born too late to taste that success. Lou Boudreau, Satchel Paige and Bob Feller, the names echoed through my childhood, ghosts whispering that this year—1968, 1972, 1975—could be the year, our year, a reprise of 1948. But it was hard to believe, sitting in the half-empty, cavernous stadium, that the Indians had ever been that good.

My mother once told me of visiting the Great Lakes Exposition, a mini World's Fair, held downtown on Cleveland's mall in the mid-1930s, along with thousands of other folks from around the nation. Then there was the great parade after the Indians championship, a decade later. Yet when I was growing up there were no great celebrations, no eruptions of civic pride—only explosions of rage, and sighs of disappointment, which seemed to mirror those in my own life.

Each day after school I'd come home, grab the Cleveland Press, the city's afternoon daily, glance at the headlines and devour the sports pages. The headlines spoke of riots down in the city—the frustration of black folks boiling over during the hot summer of 1966. The National Guard was called in, and several people were killed as fires raged through the Hough neighborhood.

The next year, in 1967, Carl Stokes was elected the first black mayor of a major American city. Watching the new mayor on TV—a good-looking man with a well-tended mustache—I felt a sense of hope mixed with pride. But within a few years, Stokes got mired in scandal and left the city, defeated. Meanwhile, Cleveland seemed to fold into itself, as factories closed, jobs were lost, and the sports teams carried on their losing traditions. Lake Erie was declared "dead," and the city earned a new nickname—"The mistake on the lake."

In 1969, before I went off to camp, I took a summer school course, obeying my mother's dictum—"Get out of the house, you're driving me crazy." For several weeks, my classmates and I visited Cleveland's attractions. We went to NASA's Lewis Research Center out at Hopkins Airport, to President James Garfield's tomb at Lake View Cemetery, and to Hough Bakery on the city's edge, where they made all the birthday cakes, their white boxes and blue lettering a staple of any gathering. In the factory, women in hairnets and white jackets bustled about. I was assaulted by the sickly-sweet smell of frosting as a line of identical white cakes rolled by, ready to be boxed and fanned out all over Greater Cleveland.

Late at night, back at home in Beachwood, I'd listen to Sportsline, a radio call-in show hosted by Pete Franklin, an opinionated man with a strong Boston accent. The show was sponsored by CEI—The Cleveland Electric Illuminating

Company—whose slogan, "Cleveland: The Best Location in the Nation," resonated throughout my childhood. In the 1940s, it may have been true. But by the late '60s, the slogan seemed half-hearted, ironic.

That June, the Cuyahoga River caught fire, proving that in Cleveland, oil and water, like Black and White, were a flammable mixture. For years, and decades afterward, the city became the butt of comedians' jokes, known only for our burning river and polluted lake.

Still, Cleveland was more than that to me. It was excursions with my grandmother Leblang, whom I called Nanny Frida, and who lived in a tiny bungalow just inside the city limits. Riding the CTS rapid train, sleek and metallic, was a novelty for a suburban boy like me. Nanny, armed with her blue and green transit schedules, would plan our excursions to Hopkins Airport, to watch the jets take off, their engines rumbling in our ears, or to see a movie like "Thoroughly Modern Millie" at one of the great theaters in Playhouse Square, soon to close. Then we'd head to the May Company Department Store, to the seventh floor toy department, where I could pick out any little thing I wanted.

On other Saturdays, I'd travel with my grandfather Cohen, Papa Ben, to Slavic Village in another corner of the city. There I'd stand behind the high wooden counter of Papa's store and sell cigarettes and Polish newspapers to the steelworkers and their wives, men and women who had been visiting Harvard Drug for a generation. As I worked, the scent of coal or ash reminded me that Cleveland was about making things—steel ingots, ball bearings, trucks and cars—that traveled around the world.

As the city emptied, suburbs like Beachwood filled up. By the time I was in high school, the vacant lots were filled by newer, larger, homes. I'd given up my attempts to play team sports, to fit in among the popular boys at my high school. I had my own interests—listening to rhythm and blues music on CKLW, the powerhouse station in Windsor, Ontario; playing tennis and trying, unsuccessfully, to develop a good serve; and counting down the days until I could leave my small suburb and create a new identity for myself in college. At Northwestern University, no one would know, or care, that as a short, scrawny teenager, I was bullied and picked on by one particular fat kid all through middle school. No one would know that while I dated girls, I dreamed of boys.

In 1975, I left home for college in Chicago. While I was away, Cleveland slid into bankruptcy, the first American city to do so since the Great Depression. Still, after earning my degree in Deaf Education, unsure of where to start my teaching career and missing old friends, I came back home. I soon found a job at A.G. Bell, Cleveland's school for deaf children. The city schools had been paralyzed by a long, bitter teachers' strike and one of their teachers had left town. Hard feelings remained, and anyone who could afford to send their children to private or suburban schools, did.

Around that time, the Plain Dealer, Cleveland's morning newspaper, came up with a new slogan: "New York may be the Big Apple, but Cleveland is a plum." The locals read the slogan on the side of city buses and laughed. How pathetic to mention Cleveland in the same sentence as New York City. How sad, to try to be something we weren't.

Cleveland was not a plum, we knew, but something more bitter, and underneath that sweet. The city was more like anise—the taste of hopes passed on and passed over to the next generation, whether they remained in town—or left, like I did, but never forgot where they came from.

Judah Leblang

Me with balloons, 1962

Me, Alex, Doug and "Dodo" 1962

THE HISTORY OF MY NAMES

I don't have just one name. The accident of my birth
provided my parents with the opportunity to give me first,
middle and last names, as well as a Hebrew name that was really
an afterthought. The names they chose have shaped my life
and bound me to their dreams, the visions of immigrants and
immigrants' children growing in the new world of America.

My names reflect the blend of cultures that have
touched my life. Bruce Edward Leblang was the big name given
to a little boy born in the suburbs of Cleveland in the late 1950s.
Bruce, a Scottish name with no relationship to the insular
Jewish world in which I grew up, was chosen for its simplicity.
My father hated being called Billy; he preferred William and
accepted Bill. Edward was selected to honor my father's father,
a Hungarian immigrant who died two years before my birth.

Leblang was handed down from this same grandfather, whom I knew only through pictures and dreams. He was described to me as a Hungarian cowboy who loved horses and farms, out of place in the fast-paced world of a big city. When my father was growing up, "Papa Ed" worked as a custodian and was often unemployed. Unfortunately, cowboys weren't needed in Depression-era Cleveland.

Leblang means "live long" in German, but men in my family usually don't. Instead they tend to die young, but look good doing it. Papa Ed, whom I know as the smiling man in a yellowed 1950s photo, died of a brain tumor at 62. My father, a workaholic who never reformed, had his first heart attack at 44, quadruple-bypass surgery at 60, and a second fatal heart attack a year later.

I missed my grandfather while growing up; I was curious to know this man my father both respected and scorned. The respect came from Papa Ed's quiet authority and determination to survive and support his family in his adopted homeland, the scorn from my father's shame when Papa worked as a custodian at the same junior high where Dad went to school.

I never fully understood the strange land called Hungary that my Nanny Frida, Papa Ed's wife, spoke of often when I

was a small boy—a land of rolling hills, whitewashed villages
and crumbling medieval castles in the foothills of the Tatra
Mountains. After her death, I wondered how my grandparents'
ancestors had come upon our family name, a label not usually
connected with Jewish people. Did they intermarry in the
cauldron of Eastern Europe? Did they originally come from
France, as some of our cousins have claimed? The answers
are lost in the mists of time and the ashes of my family who
remained in Europe, consumed in fires of hate.

I was introduced to my Hebrew name at age six, when
I started Sunday school at Park Synagogue. Though my parents
were not 'observant,' getting some training in the checkered
history of our people was a given, not a choice. On my mother's
instructions, I was given the name of Baruch, which means
"blessed." Years later, Mom claimed she had mixed up my name
with that of my younger brother, so that he became Avraham, or
Abraham, instead of me. Eventually, I put my Hebrew, English
and German names together and realized I was "Blessed Edward
Livelong," which will hopefully protect me from the various
tragedies—pogroms, spells of depression, and early death—
which dog my family.

My next birthday is soon to arrive and I've reached the
stage where my hourglass is running a bit low on sand. I know

that I will not have a son; I will not pass on my family name to a new generation. In my forties, I miss my own father and the European relatives I never met.

As I age and grow, I still remain my parents' son. Yet the names they chose for me no longer fit. I stand like a teenager in old jeans, my feet and ankles splayed out as I explore new worlds—yoga, communal living, group and talk therapy—which my parents never knew.

The old names are part of my past. I will discard some of them. I am not Hungarian, Scottish or German. But the blood of my father and mother, and their fathers and mothers, flows in my veins, in an unbroken line leading back to biblical times.

And now, Bruce is not my name.

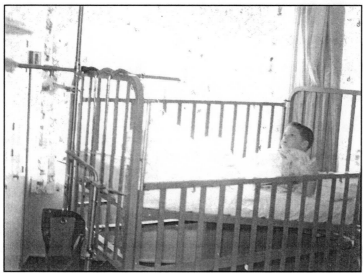

Me at Suburban Hospital, September 1962

THE OTHER SIDE

September 5, 1962. My first day of school is embedded
in my memory like a bug trapped in amber.

*

My mother, who had just earned her driver's license,
carefully piloted our orange Mercury Comet station wagon over
the half-mile distance from our house to Canterbury School,
her lacquered nails tapping the steering wheel as we approached
the immensity of the playground and ball yard. I'd been invited,
along with the other boys and girls in my kindergarten class, for
a 'meet and greet' session, the day before classes were to begin.

We filed in quietly, clutching the hands of our mothers, nervously scoping out our new classroom. Under the hum of fluorescent lights, the sights of the school absorbed me—the green linoleum floor, the beige window shades, and the commanding presence of my new teacher, Mrs. Ullner, a prune-faced woman with gray-black hair stiff as an iron rod and oversized cat's eye glasses that gave her face an owlish appearance. A warm breeze blew through the open windows, adding the scent of freshly cut grass to the institutional aroma of ammonia mixed with Comet.

"By the end of September, you will know these by heart." Gesturing with a wooden pointer, her posture stiff as her hair, Mrs. Ullner read her classroom rules out loud. The rules, which none of us could read, included reminders like, "Do not run in the classroom," "Raise your hands and not your voice," and "Act like young ladies and gentlemen." Sitting on the brown oval-shaped rug in one corner of the small classroom, I felt as if my chest and navel were trading places. How could I spend month after month with this old lady?

Knowing that I had no choice, I kept my doubts to myself. After the meeting ended, we rode over to Scott's Five and Dime, where my mother bought me a bottle of blow-bubbles, a box of Ju Ju Fruits, and a yellow plastic whistle.

When we got back home, my mother described the plan she'd devised to get me safely to and from school. We lived at 3665 Silsby Road, on a busy two-lane street I'd have to cross on a daily basis. Each morning, Mom would guide me to the other side, and then go back home to take care of my baby brother Alex, who was barely a year old, while I walked on alone. (My older brother Doug, who also attended Canterbury, was a fifth-grader with no interest in escorting me to school. If my parents asked, he would have flat out refused.) In the afternoons, I'd reach the far side of Silsby, toot my whistle, and once again, my mother would usher me to safety.

An hour later, after we returned from the dime store where I got the plastic whistle, I stood on the sidewalk across the street from home, feeling my heart skip and pump. My mother had told me I needed to practice crossing the street, signaling her with my new whistle. Soon Mom, clad in a red vinyl jacket, entered our house, closed the creaky front door and disappeared behind its diamond-shaped windows while I stood on the street. I squeezed the whistle, felt its plastic weightlessness, its impotence and silence. Looking around for another adult, someone to protect me, I spotted a gardener mowing the lawn behind me; I heard the thrum of his lawnmower, smelled its gasoline. Someone I could ask for help—the thought passed through my mind—but I dismissed it quickly, knowing, as a big boy, I should do this alone.

My mother lay across a chasm, which seemed to widen as I waited, ten or twenty seconds, an eternity. Then, launched by adrenaline, I bolted into the street, stretching for the other side. A green Pontiac, complete with fins, swooshed by and then I was flying spinning sinking, dropping onto asphalt, my left hip shattered and my mind numb.

*

I woke in a crib-like hospital bed, my left leg hung skyward at a 45-degree angle, in traction to prevent movement. Even my head was locked in place—I'd sustained a concussion, too. But my head healed quickly, and soon I could sit halfway up and examine the hospital ward where I was marooned. The children's ward of Suburban Hospital was a long narrow room with two rows of beds on opposite walls, the residents facing each other. Encased in whitenesss, surrounded by rows of beds and sheets, I didn't find much to capture my attention—other than the boy who slept in the bed next to mine.

The boy, named Roger, had been diagnosed with "walking pneumonia," which, from what I could determine,

enabled him to do anything he wanted—short of going home.
Since I couldn't move around, I exercised my imagination, with
Roger as my muse. Besides watching Shari Lewis and Lambchop,
and Kukla, Fran and Ollie, we made our own fun by inventing
a game called "Tarzan Treehouse." Inspired by the movies that
popped up on the ever-present television that sat on a ledge
above our beds, the game involved scary adventures in which
Roger played Tarzan and I became Jane. Over the past year,
I'd developed a strange fascination with that beefy man in a
loincloth, my 'member' standing at attention whenever he swung
onto the screen.

During our games, I wove stories of adventure, inspiring
Roger to save me from evil white hunters—usually Germans—
who attacked our jungle home or abducted Cheetah. Cooking
and cleaning like my Mom did for my Dad, I sautéed elephant
and stewed rhinoceros. But Roger, unlike my father, never
complained about the home cooked meals I served up with a
flourish.

After a few weeks, the ward began to empty as the kids
with tonsillitis, rubella and chicken pox went home, until only
Roger and I remained. Soon I learned that my friend was going
home, too, leaving me alone with my Tarzan movies. Roger's

parents—his father decked out in a brown wool suit, his mother dolled up like Donna Reed in a shiny beige dress and matching shoes, were packing Roger's things while his doctor "took a last listen" to my roommate's bony chest. "Hmmm," the doctor said; there was a rattle, a slight wheeze. I almost shouted with relief; my friend would be with me until the end.

The days ran together, time marked by my father's visits, his big hands tousling my hair, his gifts of Lance butter cookies and tart-tasting Pez candies in their clown dispensers from the hospital gift shop. Mom came by each afternoon, her face creased with worry, and Roger and I played our games and spun our stories. Finally, in October I went into surgery, was released from traction and put into a long plaster cast, which covered my left leg like a sleeve.

A few days later, it was my turn to go home. Roger walked near my wheelchair as Dad steered me toward the parking lot. Picking me up like a particularly valuable sack of groceries, my father stowed me in the back of our station wagon while Roger stood in the doorway, waving. My throat closed as we pulled away, and I waved back to my shrinking friend until he was no longer visible. I would not see him again.

Propped up in the living room, so I wouldn't have to tackle the stairs, I surveyed our pale beech wood furniture, the aqua blue ottoman and pink sectional sofa. Dust motes spiraled over the gray light of our television, my babysitter. Mom busied herself looking after Doug and Alex, who was just beginning to walk and talk, while my father worked six days a week, establishing his electrical contracting business. At his office just east of downtown, Dad poured over blueprints, made bids, and fought for the right to put electrical wiring into the big steel mills along the Cuyahoga River.

Eventually, I freed myself from my hospital bed and scooted around the floors of our house, watched over by my mother and our latest cleaning lady. A few days before Halloween, a surgeon finally removed my cast. Cutting the white casing in two, the doctor exposed my yellow-white left leg for the first time in seven weeks. I gasped. The withered limb had shrunk to half the width of my 'good one.'

At first I could not walk. My leg ached, and my muscles seemed unable to support my weight. But on the night before Halloween, determined to get my share of candy, I pushed myself up against our pink sofa and stumbled to a standing position. Lurching around the living room like a kindergartner who had too much Passover wine, I called out to show my parents. The following night Dad guided me out the door, as I carefully climbed my neighbors' stoops, a miniature reflection of Zorro. I greedily collected Clark bars, Chunkies and Necco wafers, allowing my father to carry me to the last few houses, when my rubbery leg wouldn't support me, when I was too tired to walk.

*

No one welcomed me back into the world of kindergarten. Mrs. Ullner made no mention of the accident, and showed little concern for my adjustment. By December, I walked to school alone—panting, sweating, crying. I had no nightmares, only fear, a constant terror that propelled me faster during every trip to and from school, a fear that I would not find my way home, that I would be lost forever.

*

One morning in March, I smelled the scent of wet grass and daffodils as I raced toward school, breathless. Mrs. Ullner chatted with another teacher as I ran into the familiar antiseptic space of our classroom, safe at last. Blinking from behind her glasses, she regarded me with skepticism or something worse.

"Here's that crybaby—the one I was telling you about," she said, gesturing in my direction. "None of the other boys or girls cry. What's wrong with you?"

I said nothing; it was hard enough just to breathe. Instead, I ate her words like sand. I had been weighed, judged, found wanting. My teacher had confirmed my fears—I was truly different than everyone else. The whole thing was my fault.

*

It was 1962, and five-year-old boys walked to school alone, did not cry, and did not dream of a boy named Roger.

Judah Leblang

Dad early 1960's

Mom

SUNDAYS IN THE POOL WITH DAD

I would be up early, bored before my parents and younger brother had plodded downstairs, and so I'd tune in Davey and Goliath, a bible-themed children's show, or Ernest Angley's, the television evangelist with a glittery smile that seemed as false as his toupee, even to my nine-year-old eyes. Angley's attempts to cure young deaf children were both riveting and futile; I knew my Uncle Jerry's deafness could not be fixed or conquered. The preacher cupped a young boy's ears in his oily palms, and said, in his southern drawl, "Say bay-bee." Then Angley shouted, "Boo!" with a theatrical clap, as if to scare away the hearing impairment, and the poor kid mumbled "buh-buh" in his still-broken speech.

As a young boy of nine or ten, I imagined God up on his throne somewhere in the sky, looking like Rex Humbard, an

Akron-based televangelist with his own Sunday morning show, as he monitored my transgressions: not cleaning up after our dog Dodo in the backyard, complaining about my 50-cent weekly allowance, or goofing off during Hebrew school. My parents didn't seem to have much faith in a higher power of any stripe, and my Hebrew-school teachers didn't tell me what God looked like—you weren't even allowed to pronounce His name.

Once Angley's act had ended, I'd grab the Cleveland Plain Dealer from our front steps and rummage through the inky blackness of its headlines: race riots and burned-out homes on the city's East Side, troop build-ups in Vietnam, LBJ's "War on Poverty," until I found my prize—the sports section. There I could savor the Ohio State Buckeyes' latest football victory over their hapless Big Ten rivals from other Midwestern states, or mourn the Cleveland Indians' latest loss, their futile quest to break .500.

My mother would walk down the stairs, say, "Morning dear," and take the carpet sweeper from the hall closet, soon to be followed by the vacuum cleaner. Seven-thirty on Sunday morning was a bit too early to run machinery, but not much. The sweeper would roll across the foyer rug, the feather duster tickling the furniture in the living room my brothers and I could not enter, except on holidays and special occasions, and then my mother would be vacuuming, a not so subtle way of getting everyone in the house up and at 'em.

Eventually, my father would stomp downstairs, grumble something that might mean hello, and head for the kitchen, his joints cracking. Seeing him, Mom would put the instant hot water from our special tap into Dad's instant Taster's Choice frozen coffee, and place it before him in a green ceramic mug. He'd remain mute, as always, before his first cup. Then she would put out the bagels, I'd grab the lox—a Sunday-only treat—out of the fridge, and we'd munch our poppy-seed and onion bagels in silence.

Gradually my father would gain speech and reach for the newspaper—first sports, then news. Later, toward afternoon, we'd pile into his leather-seated Oldsmobile for our weekly excursion. Dad, a bit impatient, but always in control while driving, manned the wheel while my mother, the assigned navigator, mapped our route.

I'd try not to think about Monday—I often dreaded school—confrontations with bullies like Marty Simberg, who chased me home and threatened to beat me up every week for five years. I focused on our road trips instead, out east into the rolling hills of Amish country, dour-looking men and their plain-dressed wives guiding their horses and buggies down two-lane Ohio roads. Or down into the city for special events—a trip to our grand white-pillared art museum, with Rodin's Thinker out front; the Crawford Auto Museum where my dad and I both drooled over mint condition antique cars from the early 1900s, Duryeas, Packards and Pierce-Arrows, boxy silver or sleek black; or downtown to the Cleveland Browns games at Municipal Stadium, where my father had season tickets on the goal line, the old structure shaking under the feet of 85,000 football fans.

In small-town Ohio, there were festivals for every season, and over time, we visited most of them. In spring, there was the Maple Syrup Festival, where I gobbled stacks of pancakes, my fingers sticky, mouth puckered and sweet for hours afterward, and the Butter Churn Festival, with its thick butter and fresh cream, both in nearby Geauga County. In summer and fall came the county fairs, each 'the biggest and best,' along with the Pumpkin Festival down in Circleville, which featured pumpkin bread, candy, the largest pumpkin pie ever made, and the biggest pumpkin I'd ever seen—a massive rust-colored blob, weighing in at almost 1,000 pounds.

My favorite trips brought us to the water. Though my mother, with her red hair and fair complexion, avoided both beach and sun, I could usually persuade my father to squire us to the water—to Cedar Point, the great amusement park with a beach on Lake Erie—for a few days each summer, or for afternoon excursions, to Lake Plata, a concrete-floored, oval-shaped 'pond' with a grass beach southeast of Cleveland, near Kent. There, in the mid-late 1960s, my younger brother Alex, Dad and I would 'horse around' in the chlorinated water, my mother reading "Mandingo" or another romance novel in the grassy shade, while Doug was off visiting friends back in Beachwood.

In the pool, Dad wore one of his baggy olive-plaid bathing suits, his broad shoulders, arms and legs matted with coarse black hair. My father crouched, and I'd climb onto his sturdy thighs and push off, using him as a human springboard. Tucking my limber child's frame, I'd fly through the summer air, stomach flipping as I dropped down into the man-made lake and swam back for another round, until we'd both had enough. My father visibly relaxed, and for a few hours, I could see the boy he still carried within him, the one who loved bad puns and silly jokes.

On those Sundays, I'd relax, drop my guard, and forget how my father's moods could shift suddenly, like the winds over Lake Erie. Once, near another pool in Avon Lake, my father pushed and tickled me, until, spouting one of the grown-up phrases I'd heard at day camp, I told him to "cut the crap."

Suddenly, I found myself swinging several feet off the ground, my father's right hand painfully clamped around my neck as he held me aloft, shaking me as he said, "Don't-you-ever-use-that-word-again!" Stunned and unsure what the world actually meant, I felt tears spring to my eyes.

I didn't swear in front of my parents until, home for the summer after my freshman year of college, riding in the back seat of my father's latest Lincoln and looking at how Alex had grown, I said, "Shit, you've got big feet" and, catching myself, "um…I mean you've got large feet." My parents locked eyes in the front seat, and burst out laughing. Evidently, I'd finally come of age.

Ravenous after swimming, I'd tear into the picnic supper my mother had assembled in our Styrofoam cooler. Potato salad and sliced turkey from Heinen's Grocery served between sliced Jewish rye from Pincus Bakery, rich with caraway seeds, sweet peaches or watermelon slices for dessert, the juice dripping on my swimsuit, washed down with small cans of Hawaiian Punch.

Another hour or two passed; my mother reminded us to get going. Sometime later, we'd pull into our narrow driveway, face the white brick colonial with its black and white awnings, and enter the coolness of our air-conditioned kitchen.

And then began our Sunday night routine. Dad pointed us upstairs, and Alex and I clambered toward my parents' white-tiled stall shower, with its frosted glass door and a small ledge where you could sit down if you got tired. Their bathroom was usually off-limits, and filled with grown-up scents like my father's Old Spice aftershave and my mother's Noxzema face cream and L'Air du Temps perfume.

Slipping into the steamy cubicle, I'd lose myself in the spray. My father soaped me up, massaging head, shoulders and back, working in the shampoo until my scalp buzzed, and then placed me under the showerhead for a full rinse and towel dry. Fully clean, I'd slide into the soft white pajamas handed down from Doug that looked like a baseball uniform, full of the balls I couldn't hit or catch.

Rubbery, I'd float downstairs and sprawl out on our '60s modern rug, its blue and green triangles marking my assigned space before our new Zenith color TV, to watch a talking horse and then a host, both named Ed. My father would appear in his gray pajamas, a few minutes later, while my mother sat in her usual spot on the couch behind me, filing her crimson nails.

As evening turned to night, my mother drew the drapes closed. I'd lose myself in the colored light of Ed Sullivan and Topo Gigio, feeling the four of us knit together as a family, if only for this one day and night.

Nanny Frida, me, early 1960s

THE WONDERS OF CLEVELAND

My mother steered our brown Pontiac through suburban Beachwood toward Nanny's house, on the edge of working-class Cleveland. I fidgeted on the vinyl seat, my body an unspoken "Are we there yet?" Finally, we passed into the city and my mother stopped in front of the tall maple that dominated my grandmother's postage-stamp-sized front lawn. Nanny's tiny bungalow sat in a row of identical white houses thrown up just after World War II when Cleveland was booming, years before my birth.

My mother waved to Nanny, her mother-in-law, and told me, "I'll be back at five o'clock sharp. Keep an eye on the time and stay with your grandmother."

I mumbled, "OK, Mom," and began to salivate like one of Pavlov's dogs, knowing that Nanny would have baked the long, sweet poppyseed rolls she called "mun," a taste of her native Hungary.

My grandmother pulled me in as I reached the front steps, her blue-gray eyes beaming. I felt the soft warmth of her flesh, smelled her scent of Vicks lemon cough drops mixed with baby powder.

"So Nanny, are we going into town?" I asked, and a smile dusted her face like powdered sugar.

"No sure not," she said, Hungarian-English for 'of course.'

I knew my parents didn't like the city. My mother saw Cleveland as a cauldron of riots, crime and burned out neighborhoods, a place to avoid. Still, on a sunny day in May 1968, I was an eleven-year-old boy who knew that Cleveland was full of wonders like planes and trains and buildings that pierced the sky, miracles my grandmother and I would share like her warm pastry. And so Nanny and I stood quietly as my mother drove off, back to the safety of the eastern suburbs.

Waiting for the bus, Nanny's maple tree rustling
above us, I thought of other times, other adventures with
my grandmother, when I was five, seven, eight. On special
weekends, she would baby-sit for my brothers and me, bringing
her pastry and her Jewish rye bread, her cough drops and
powdery scent into our suburban home. At five, before the
accident, I'd sing and dance for her entertainment, repeating
rhymes I'd learned in nursery school—"Mary Had a Little
Lamb," "Humpty Dumpty," and later, "My Country 'Tis of
Thee," which I'd warbled at a school assembly in kindergarten in
my thin childish voice. Later, I'd tell my grandmother she was
beautiful, and promise to marry her when I grew up. According
to my mother, I was a little khnifenik—Yiddish for a "flatterer."

Soon we boarded the CTS Windermere-bound bus,
where we'd catch the "rapid-transit" train, and Nanny greeted
the driver. Sitting on the front bench seat, I felt the weight of
my grandmother's presence—thick arms and legs, skin lined
and freckled, her thick wrist encircled by a gold watchband, feet
encased in sensible black, wide-heeled shoes. I imagined her as
the young, determined woman who pushed my grandfather,
Papa Ed, to leave Hungary after the First World War. "I was the
one who wanted to leave Europe—he wanted to stay home and
ride horses," she said, shaking her head at the silliness of the idea.

I never met my grandfather, but my mind filled with images of a Hungarian-Jewish cowboy—Roy Rogers with a skullcap.

An hour later, we were at Cleveland Hopkins International Airport. I roamed among the ticket counters, picking up timetables for Mohawk, Allegheny and United Airlines. Later, we stood on the observation deck, breathed in the heady aroma of jet fuel, and craned our necks as the metallic tubes threaded the clouds. The scent powered my dreams of a trip to Florida—my parents had promised me my first flying vacation the following December. "Enough noise!" my grandmother yelled above the din as she pulled me back inside the terminal.

Another Rapid train deposited us into the flurry of downtown Cleveland, at Euclid Avenue and Public Square. A haze drifted over from the steel mills down on the Cuyahoga River, coating the air with fine dust and ashes. Hungry, I led the way down Euclid Avenue, Cleveland's bustling main street, toward the lunch counter at Woolworth's. There I'd have my favorite lunch—two slices of pepperoni pizza and an orange drink.

When we arrived, Nanny started up a conversation with another gray-haired lady sitting on a nearby stool. "Yes, this is my grandson, we're *exploring* for the day," she said, emphasizing the word as if we were on a secret assignment for LBJ. The other lady nodded, impressed, and blood rushed to my face. I looked down and mumbled, "Let's go Nanny." I knew I wasn't that special.

A five-minute walk back down Euclid brought us to the faded art-deco splendor of the Terminal Tower, the tallest building in all of Cleveland. As we walked among the half-empty stores on the Terminal's ground floor, we came upon the old train station, its yellowed wooden benches empty, hallways echoing. The station, according to my grandmother, was once "packed with people." Now, just a handful sat on the pale wooden benches, a few travelers to the "best location in the nation."

Hmm. I gazed at the grand WPA mural that filled a wall of the waiting area—a dramatic drawing of the men who built the Terminal, steelworkers sitting on metal beams, strong men with bulging muscles, their faces proud. They erected this 700-foot tall building—the tallest between New York and Chicago—that looked out over Lake Erie, complete with an observation deck on the 42nd floor. I felt a twinge of jealousy, knowing I'd never see a new Terminal Tower or feel the excitement of a championship baseball team, only air tinged with coal dust and losing teams in our old industrial city.

Our last stop was at the May Company Department Store for a "frosty." A thick ice cream and chocolate milkshake served in a narrow Coke-style glass, the frosty was the coup de grace of our visits to downtown Cleveland. Leaning against the Formica counter in the basement of the old store, I guzzled the thick liquid beige liquid and rubbed my forehead as my ice cream-induced headache began to spread. Nanny shook her head, laughed, and sipped her frosty, an adult who knew better.

The day rolled to a slow, gentle end as we rode the train and bus back toward my grandmother's house. I rocked to the rhythm of the CTS Rapid train, my mouth still buzzing with the taste of cold chocolate. Near Windermere, my head nodded forward and I shook myself awake, determined not to miss one minute of our time together.

Sometime later, the bus pulled up in front of Nanny's bungalow. My mother waited, sitting in our brown station wagon, tapping the steering wheel. Her auburn hair was teased into a bangy-bouffant '60s style, so in contrast to the thin gray curls of my grandmother. Nanny waved to her daughter-in-law and rushed into the house. Before I reached the front steps,

Nanny returned with two packages wrapped in aluminum foil. I knew the log-shaped one was filled with the black nectar of poppyseeds, the smaller with nut cookies for Alex.

"Thank your grandmother," my mother called out from the car. I shrugged, knowing I didn't need to say anything, that we were connected in a place beyond words. I hugged Nanny once more, careful not to let her crush my packages. Then I walked toward my mother, who was chewing a fingernail, anxious to leave.

As we drove away, Nanny stood on the front stoop, unsmiling. I watched her standing there as we rode home, following me with her blue-gray eyes, guarding me until we were out of sight.

Judah Leblang

Me at home, 1968

TRACING MY WAY HOME

We pulled up before the faded stone of the Ohio
College of Podiatry building on East 105th and Carnegie, on the
edge of Cleveland's East Side ghetto. Moving toward Doctor
Rosenthal's office, my stomach turned as if I were on the edge of
an abyss, about to jump.

Throat cultures, fevers, swollen glands—my years-long
battle with strep throat raged on. On this day, in November of
1969, my mother led the way into the waiting room, all dark
wood and murals from the 1930s. The room smelled antiseptic,
a mix of ammonia, piss and fear, the scents I associated with

53

Doctor Rosenthal. Winnie the Pooh and friends cavorted on the doctor's walls, fading with time like the old man himself. I scanned the small play area jumbled with toys from my mother's day. A Raggedy Ann doll looked up at me, forlorn. I stared back, my gut twisting, until I heard the doctor's phlegmy German voice seep out of his office, hard vowels and mucous bubbling in his throat like Listerine.

Fidgeting in the waiting room, I paged through Reader's Digest, glancing at pictures of two boys hanging onto a sailboat in a storm. I thought of their courage as I paced the room, back and forth, trying to slow my pounding heart. "One throat culture, no big deal," I whispered to myself. My mother sat and read one of her thick paperback novels, eyes moving left to right as she read. She was engrossed in a romance—I could tell from the full-bodiced woman swooning on the front cover—while I waited, enmeshed in a nightmare. Soon Doctor Rosenthal would be upon me, his gray gloves and tongue depressor at the ready.

Eventually, Mom looked up from her book and sighed. "Can't you just grab a toy and play like the other kids? You're making me a nervous wreck!" She shook her head and sighed again, as if I were beyond redemption—as if she wouldn't be just as anxious without me.

She returned to her tropical island, lost in a better place. I noticed her rose-colored lipstick had smudged, leaving a residue on her slightly uneven front teeth. I was twelve years old, too old to be playing with the Raggedy Ann dolls and Lincoln logs the doctor provided for his victims.

The doctor beckoned us from the examining room. My mother followed behind, cutting off my escape route. He smiled; I shook his roughened palm and met his washed-out blue eyes with my own, knowing what was coming. As he gurgled, "How are you, young mahhn?" I backed away, ready for our ritual dance. He reached up toward my neck with his disfigured hands, fingernails worn away by X-ray radiation in the early 1900s, in his native Austria.

The doctor's gray gloves, cut at the knuckles, exposed his nail-less fingers as he pressed my throat, explored my glands. "Um hmmm," he mumbled, and I knew my glands were swollen as they always were, as they had been for years. Then Doctor Rosenthal pulled out a tongue depressor as wide as my wrist and began to tunnel deep inside my throat. Instinctively, I raised my hands, pulled at his hairy arm as he prepared to push toward my uvula.

"Say ahh," he commanded, as I choked and pushed against him.

"Sit on your hands!" he barked and we began round two, my mother pushing on my shoulders to keep me on the gray stool as the doctor grabbed another swab.

This time he went in quickly—lightning strike. I jerked my head, gagged, and it was over. My eyes teared and a bolt of sunlight seared my blood 'til it wanted to boil. I wanted to kill the old Nazi and my mother along with him. Of course, I knew he was not a Nazi but a Jew like me. Still, I hated him, his hateful accent and his yellow teeth.

My mother left the room and the rest of the exam went quickly, a prod here, a cough there. There were no shots on this day, a good thing, as I screamed at the sight of a needle. Doctor Rosenthal was a stickler for vaccines, immunizations, preventive medicine. I was averse to invasive procedures.

I simply wanted to be left alone, to dream through the books I loved, my travel books. Those books—"Fielding's Travel Guide to Europe," "Fodor's Guide," "Europe on 25 Dollars a Day"—took me to exotic places far removed from suburban Cleveland, where people spoke languages like French and Icelandic and didn't squirm through Hebrew School or struggle with scary German doctors who choked them with tongue depressors.

Doctor Rosenthal waddled up to my mother, wearing his yellow grin like a rictus. Barely her height—just five feet tall—his bald head was framed by ears infested with white hairs. "He still has dah strep throat," the doctor mumbled, writing out a prescription on his dusty pad, his handwriting spidery like the Hebrew letters I saw in temple. My mother sighed again, a martyr for the cause.

"I'll have to chop them up in orange juice—he won't swallow the damn things." She was right, of course. I had a fear of choking on one of the foul-tasting tablets.

The late afternoon air grew cold as fall turned toward winter. Sinking into the passenger seat of our Pontiac Tempest station wagon, my body felt slick with sweat, relieved. The city was closing as commuters rushed toward Cedar Hill, escaping their offices and factories, leaving the old double-decker houses of Cleveland to sink below like arthritic senior citizens. We joined the line of traffic and rose up Cedar Hill toward the eastern suburbs. I tried not to think about the bitter taste of Erythromycin, the good doctor's drug of choice.

My mother looked at me and shook her head. "You just had to make a big to-do about this, didn't you? Like I don't have enough to worry about with Doug's behavior and your father complaining and Nanny Fay being sick…" The litany went on and I tried to tune out, knowing the list by heart. My older brother Doug had been caught drinking beer with friends and shipped off to a boarding school for children who "needed more structure." My "other" grandmother, Nanny Fay, was sickly, needy, dependent on my mother. My father complained when dinner was (often) not to his liking. No one appreciated my mother for the hard-working woman she was.

I was a twelve-year-old boy afraid of many things: Doctor Rosenthal, fistfights, swimming in deep water, and the feelings I got when I wrestled with my (male) friends. Closing my eyes as my mother listed the ways I'd disappointed her, her anger pinned me down into the faded fabric of the front seat. I heard the thinka-thunk of the windshield wipers and traced my way home, eyes still closed, knowing my place in the world, not expecting any more or less.

An Attack of the Heart

We never did get to New York. We went to Mt. Sinai
Hospital instead, my father in a red and white ambulance, my
mother and I in our blue Mercury Monterey. In early April
1971, just two weeks before our scheduled trip to the Big Apple,
where I, a 14-year-old boy, would finally fulfill my dream of
seeing a Broadway musical—Fiddler on the Roof or Hair—my
father suffered a massive heart attack.

A gray, rainy Sunday, my Dad was off playing in his
weekly tennis match, while I ate lunch—lox and cream cheese
on a poppyseed bagel. My mother picked up the beige wall
phone perched near her writing desk, and suddenly, voice
catching, narrow shoulders stiffening, her birdlike frame
contracted into itself. She turned to me, her face flushed,
reddened. My father had collapsed on the spongy rubber surface
of the tennis center. The bagel sat on my plate, forgotten.

Racing through the windy streets of Cleveland's East
Side toward Mt. Sinai Hospital, I wondered what we'd find, and
whether I'd have a chance to apologize for my kvetchy behavior
of the week before, when I'd pleaded for "just one more day,
Dad" in New York when he called Allegheny Airlines to make
our reservations.

My mother pulled into the garage, bit her lip, and grabbed her purse. As we ran toward the ER, I pictured my Dad in intensive care, lost in a maze of flashing lights, mechanic beeps, stainless steel, surrounded by green-garbed physicians. An engineer who dressed as he thought—square, conservative, linear—my father took up space without trying. His white shirts and mild ties, rectangular-framed glasses perched on a wide nose, and his monogrammed brown leather briefcase announced a man in control, a man who knew where things should be placed.

In the white light of the ER waiting room, it was hard to believe, according to the young white-jacketed resident who approached my mother, "We don't know if he's going to make it." I stood nearby, stiffly, trying to act like an adult as I digested the news. In my mind's eye, I heard my father's deep voice, his bone-cracking walk, so powerful, so masculine, and half-expected him—a vibrant, 44-year-old man—to come walking down the hall, smiling, as if it were all a false alarm, a terrible mistake.

We waited, watching live bodies come and go, the hum of the wounded and their loved ones. Toward evening, the doctors said my father was doing a bit better, and my mother and I rode home in silence. By the next morning, it appeared he would not die, at least not that day or week.

*

My father spent a month in the hospital, slowly working his way back, shuffling down the hallway once, then twice. At 14, I was two years too young to visit my Dad in his room, according to hospital rules. Or perhaps this was my mother's way of protecting me, of not letting me see my father in his weakened condition.

One day, after her daily visit to the hospital, I heard my mother on the phone, telling a friend that my father had cried during her visit, and said he was afraid of dying. I'd never seen my father cry, and I felt his fear—the fear of losing him, the threat of his mortality—inside my own body.

*

Several weeks later, my father returned home, driven carefully by my mother, and guided, with equal care, step by step, up the stairs to Doug's bedroom, since my older brother was away at Ohio State. Donna, the strict, churchgoing 'cleaning lady' who had come to work for my parents six years earlier, set my father up with his medications, extra pillows, blankets.

After school, I ran upstairs and there, in the gray light of afternoon, was my Dad, propped up on pillows, looking too big, with his broad shoulders and long legs, for Doug's narrow twin bed. The crooked smile, the yellowed teeth—too many years of pipe smoking and bottled soda—were still there, though he'd grown thinner, weakened from the attack and his time in the hospital. Ensconced in my brother's old room, where he could rest undisturbed, Dad read, slept, and took his Coumadin, a blood-thinning medication.

Over the past 15 years, my father's reading had consisted of the Electrical Engineering Record and Contracting Today. After his heart attack, his tastes changed to books like "I'm OK, You're OK," and "I Ain't Much Baby—But I'm All I've Got," a —rainbow-colored paperback by Jess Lair, a heart-attack victim who transformed himself into a guru for recovering Type A heart patients in the early 1970s.

My Dad fit the Type A personality to a T. A successful son of poor immigrants, the president of a mid-sized company with three boys, a shapely wife, and a four-bedroom house. Driven to succeed, to go beyond the modest achievements of his Hungarian father, my Dad labored six days a week for 20 years, providing his family with all the material things he'd never had.

Though my father's days at Lake Erie Electric were filled with deadlines, competitive bids, and management-union beefs, he claimed to enjoy his work. But sometimes, I'd heard that my father screamed at his employees, barked orders at them as he did with us, in those moments when his rage roared to the surface. It wasn't until years later that I understood my father used his work in the same way my mother used her cleaning—to control life—and to avoid the tension that baked in our house like a brisket left too long in the oven.

The heart attack did what my mother couldn't—slowed my father down, and forced him to notice that beneath his anger there were other feelings—sadness, disappointment, fear. His heart attack, my father said, "Made me think about all the things I haven't done, and realize that life is short, and you better make the most of it."

Over the next few years, I watched, as the father I knew, the strict repressed engineer who had raised me to age 14, transformed into a new, looser Dad. As he recovered, he seemed almost the same, and as time went along, increasingly different, driven beneath his longish sideburns and wire-rim glasses by a new fear—that he would run out of time, and die young.

Judah Leblang

Jerry on his second wedding day-1973

REMEMBERING JERRY

I search my uncle's face, curiously three-dimensional in a black-and-white photograph from 1961. Eyes wide open, smile broad, forehead creased, sloping into his bald domed crown, framed by big ears that didn't function. Uncle Jerry had large expressive hands that tickled me when I was a boy of six, eight, ten. I study him in the battered scrapbook my mother gave me several years ago, and imagine him and his vice-like grip reaching out across the page.

65

At six feet three inches, Jerry towered over his sister (my mother), was bigger and broader than my father. A boy wrapped in a man's body, so it seemed to me—big, strong, but slow to understand the world around him. With his deaf speech and broken ears, people struggled to understand him, or grew bored and gave up. I was used to Jerry's voice and could capture almost everything he said. But I didn't say much in response, and didn't have the patience to talk with him about his glory days—events in a distant past, years before I was born.

*

I sat in Arthur Treacher's Fish and Chips on a fall day in 1972, staring through glass at the Cleveland Heights High School athletic field across the street. A rainy Sunday, the gray gloom compounded by the smell of hot grease that permeated the fast-food restaurant. My grandfather, Papa Ben, talked with my mother, while her younger brother, my Uncle Jerry, squeezed my shoulder a bit too hard and pointed across to the schoolyard.

"I played basketball and baseball—got varsity letters, you know? Only deaf kid in the whole league." Jerry's long index finger tapped his chest, and I saw his eyes go back there, to high school in the late 1940s and early '50s. His words pelted me— flat and cool like raindrops, and sounded as if he were gargling water. I nodded and looked impressed. I knew I'd never earn a high school letter, that my best sports were tetherball and ping-pong.

As drizzle spattered the window, I wondered why my uncle still lived in his memories of twenty years earlier. If he had peaked at Heights High, if everything after was a downhill ride, what did he have to live for? He was staying with Nanny and Papa again, back home after ten years of marriage. His deaf wife, my Aunt Terri, had fled back to Illinois with their hearing daughter, Sue, after a messy divorce. Jerry didn't have any hobbies I knew of, other than watching sports on TV and dancing. He loved to dance, and felt the beat vibrate through the floor—pulsating into his size twelve shoes.

My grandfather had me nudge Jerry; he wanted my uncle's full attention. Soon I heard Papa's raspy, "How many times have I told you?" as he lectured Uncle Jerry about being a responsible adult and getting things done on time. I tuned out Papa's voice and went deaf myself, focusing instead on my grandfather's face, which had gone from taupe to rose, and watched a vein pulse in his temple, while Jerry's face turned a sick yellow-gray.

Jerry turned back to me, sighed, and pointed back across the street. I followed the arc of his long fingers, hands slicing air as he gestured. As he talked about 1950 in his craggy speech, I knew, instinctively, he was blocking out his life today, his wife and daughter living on the streets of Chicago. According to my mother, Aunt Terri was schizophrenic, and Sue was with her, wandering. After his wife and daughter left, Jerry had only his work to fill his days. An assistant draftsman, Jerry was good with his hands. On his drafting table, the world was reduced to schematic drawings and clean angled lines, pictures my uncle could decipher.

I'd never seen my uncle sign. His teachers had told him he must "overcome his handicap," must speak, read lips, and strain, always strain, until he could understand normal people— those who could hear—and he tried, mightily.

At 15, I was five feet two inches tall and painfully thin, still waiting for puberty years after my friends had arrived. I dreaded high school gym class, showing my (lack of) manhood in the locker room, and playing team sports. During spring, when gym class consisted of baseball practice, I prayed for rain, dreading my placement in the outfield, where, if a ball did fly in my direction, I'd invariably drop it or, worse, deflect it with my face. In tenth grade, when we could choose our poison, I took tennis, a game I played with some proficiency. But according to my teacher, I looked "like a ballerina," as I stretched to return the balls. I hated high school, hated being a boy who couldn't do boy things.

Sometimes, on Saturday nights, I stayed over at my grandparents' house, and Jerry and I watched wrestling. My uncle smiled and cheered; it was a dance he knew well, no captions needed. I watched the show, too, enjoying the 'sport' for different reasons—for the excitement that wended through me, sexual, forbidden.

Uncle Jerry leaned toward the black and white TV, sitting on the edge of his twin bed, his head shiny, eyes fixed on the screen. I squirmed on the other bed, keeping my shirt untucked, disguising my arousal. Raymond Rougeau and Luis Martinez squared off, a handsome young Canadian and a savvy Mexican, Rougeau in blue briefs that displayed his muscular butt, Martinez in black ones that emphasized his toughness and experience. Jerry pointed to Martinez and nodded. "He's gonna kill that boy." I rooted for the underdog—Rougeau—as he took a shot to the midsection and fell at the feet of Martinez. Transfixed by the struggle, I memorized the athletic curves of Rougeau's thighs, the ample mounds of his pecs. Meanwhile, Jerry enjoyed the contest, pretending that it was real, forgetting that it wasn't.

*

Two years later, in September 1974, I was circulating at my brother, Alex's Bar Mitzvah party at the Host House Party Center in Mayfield Heights, east of Cleveland. My parents' friends, Papa Ben and Nanny Fay, and assorted cousins from Columbus and Steubenville had gathered for the occasion. Mingling with the crowd, I collected hugs and compliments on being a high school senior and a good student. I was nearly six feet tall after growing six inches in the past year, taller than most of the men—but not Uncle Jerry. As I turned, I saw him and his second wife—a dark-haired doe-eyed woman he'd met at a party and married the previous year, head toward the band. My "new aunt," with her huge brown eyes and painted face, was a ringer for Aunt Terri, but she could hear and speak, and her name was Renee.

Jerry and Renee had a brief honeymoon period after their wedding. Now, my mother said, they were "having problems." I didn't ask for the details. But on that night, gliding to the dance floor, leading his second wife by the hand, Jerry was radiant. Renee turned to him and laughed, eyes framed by her black eyeliner and inky hair. Their hips moved side to side, my uncle spinning out with the beat, black shoes shining, fingers snapping. I picture a platinum blond with a soulful voice, belting out Aretha Franklin's "R-E-S-P-E-C-T/taking care of

TCB," and my uncle was with her, getting down, rocking out and no one could tell him that he was not whole, not full, not right for this one night....

*

I came in through the back door of my parents' house, my mind counting down the days until graduation. It was May, 1975, and in just four months I'd be leaving Cleveland—for good, I hoped—for college in Chicago. I felt a blast of air-conditioning as Alex met me in the back hallway.

"It's Uncle Jerry—he had a heart attack and was rushed to Hillcrest Hospital. He's dead."

I felt numb, suspended, my ears buzzing as if my own hearing were fading. This couldn't be happening, not to my only uncle who was 44 years old, and who finally, in the last few months, looked happy, contented. Renee had taken him to the doctor a few days earlier, when he complained of flu-like symptoms. The doctor sent him home, told him to rest. By the time he reached the hospital two days later, Jerry had suffered a heart attack.

*

A few months before Jerry died, I met an old high school friend of my mother's, who ran a school for deaf children on Cleveland's West Side. I went and visited some of her classes and saw children signing to each other, communicating with their voices and their hands. Watching those children, especially the boys, their faces animated and elastic, eyes wide, fingers drawing pictures in the air, stirred me. I wanted to learn their language, to express myself with my face, body, and hands, in the way I never could with Jerry.

*

Over the next 25 years, I worked as a teacher of the deaf, a sign language interpreter, and a career counselor with hearing students. After stints of several years, I would leave the deaf world, frustrated by the walls of language and culture that separate hearing and deaf people. But after a few years away from that world, I'd hear a small voice saying, "Go back and try again," and I would.

*

Today I finger the smooth pages of the scrapbook, which have gone yellow with age. I feel Jerry's presence, wispy as a dream that fades in the light of morning, close the book, cover my uncle's face with red cardboard and crawl back into bed, sinking into the silence he knew so well.

Papa and Me 1960

PAPA'S PLACE

My mother often said, "Your grandfather's gonna die in that store," and now, on a stifling day in July 1975, two months after Jerry's death, it appears she might be right. I press the accelerator and careen down Harvard Avenue, propelled by the scribbled note she left on the kitchen counter.

"Papa rushed to St. Alexis—collapsed at store. Hurry!" she wrote, and I do, a nervous 18-year-old steering my grandfather's rusted-out Chevy Bel Air through the Mt. Pleasant neighborhood toward Slavic Village, on Cleveland's southeast side. As I drive, I inhale the smell of tobacco that clings to anything Papa touches, his scent of Camels mixed with musk.

On special Saturdays, I rode with my grandfather to Harvard and East 71st Street, where we entered the dusty recesses of Harvard Drug, Papa's pharmacy. Once he told me of his arrival in this close-knit Polish community in the 1920s, when Jews were no more welcome than rabid dogs. But after decades of mixing medicines for the factory workers and their hard-working wives—the store was open every day for 53 years—they'd made him an honorary member of the Union of Poles, a tribute usually reserved for Polish Catholics.

*

As I near the hospital, I am 12 again, peering out from behind the front counter of the store. I stand next to the gold-plated cash register, turn its useless crank, and make change off the top, carefully counting the coins of Papa's customers as they buy their Polish newspapers, their Clark bars, their Tareyton cigarettes. The front door is usually propped open; a ceiling fan stirs the mill-dusted air.

Old folks come in for coffee, sit at the front table with my aunt as Papa and his brother, my great-uncle Itz, fill their prescriptions in back. Papa works steadily, his sleeves rolled up. I hear my name mentioned, and, one by one, the customers come over to say hello, to shake my hand or grasp my shoulder.

"Your grandfather's a fine man," one says, and I nod shyly.

As I race past Odziemski Hardware, Holy Name Catholic Church, and Kormorowski's Funeral Home, I imagine Papa laid out at Berkowitz-Kumin, the Jewish funeral home in Cleveland Heights, but know his soul would be wandering here among the fading double-decker houses of "the neighborhood."

In the hospital waiting room, my mother and grandmother sit huddled on a couch. Above them, a gold cross gleams in the dim light. I know I am too late.

Papa was buried in a new cemetery out in Chesterland, far from his home in suburban Beachwood and his store in the city. Most of the locals didn't come to the funeral. They came to the store instead, recalling my grandfather over cups of coffee and slices of sweet babka, the older men smoking, their shirts sweaty in the summer heat, the women clad in babushkas.

"Ben helped us out when we couldn't pay a doctor, gave us the medicine on credit," one man said, and I knew Papa had done the same for countless others during the Depression and World War II. Meanwhile, at the front table, Uncle Itz sat mute, weak from grief and his recent stroke.

No one wanted to buy my grandfather's little business. Finally, after a month of running the store, filling prescriptions with a rotating cast of druggists, my parents sold Papa's customer list to a competitor, for $2,000. Then they brought in an auctioneer to strip the old store clean. A grizzled West Virginian with a no-nonsense manner, he had me empty the bottles of their precious liquids; soon the floor was covered with sea-green and purple glass shining in the dusky light. Sometime later, the building was destroyed, and with it, all traces of my grandfather.

*

Twenty-five years later, I returned to the neighborhood. Now integrated, blacks and whites walked sidewalks cracked and edgy, past storefronts, some empty, others with new names and owners. A few—a camping supply store, a Polish restaurant— remained from Papa's day. Taking it all in, I sat in a coffee shop half a block from the old store, a brighter, remodeled version of the greasy spoon Papa and I visited on the way into work—him for coffee black, me for a coconut crème donut. Then we'd walk half a block to Harvard Drug, Papa leading, me trailing in a cloud of his blue smoke.

The proprietor, a balding newcomer to the neighborhood, didn't know my grandfather, but the old woman who shuffled by, rosy-cheeked, her head covered by a pink

babushka, probably did. As I stood in the parking lot of a
new Rite Aid drug store, where Papa's pharmacy used to be, I
pictured the old woman buying candy as a young girl, greeting
Uncle Itz and my grandfather under the lazy ceiling fan, Aunt
Lottie making change from the broken, gilded register.

The old woman approached the Rite Aid, walking
slowly. The doors opened with a pneumatic whoosh and
the woman was sucked inside, into the brightly-lit, well-
organized store, where no one sits, drinks coffee or reads Polish
newspapers.

FINDING MY OWN PLACE

PART TWO

WHAT A FELLOWSHIP

In August 1997, I made a special visit back to Cleveland
to represent my family at a memorial service for my godmother
Donna's son Lonnie, who had died two years earlier. Since
Lonnie had been a member of the little church where Donna
was a "mother" and senior member, the service was doubling
as an afternoon fundraiser. The goal of the congregation—one
they were moving toward in tiny increments, year by year—was
to connect their modest sanctuary with the warehouse-like
building next door, tearing down the wall between them. The
second building, which served as a reception hall, was really just
a large, concrete-floored room, looking desperate for paint and a
makeover, like the ugly duckling at a high school dance.

The day before the big event, Donna asked me to say a
few words at the service. Though I barely knew Lonnie, I could
speak of knowing Donna, who had worked for my family as a
'cleaning lady' from the time I was 8 until I was pushing 40.
Over time, she became my second mother, a warm accepting
presence, a source of unconditional love. It wasn't until I reached
adulthood that I recognized that Donna's rules were simply her
way of expressing caring, her way of ensuring that my younger
brother and I "turned out right." Finally, as I reached middle age,

I began to call her my godmother, and she to refer to me as her godson.

I said I'd think of something to say if it would please her. She nodded and said it would, and I started to perspire—heavily. Donna's grandchildren—Lonnie's children—would all be there, folks I'd heard of but had met only once or twice. How would they feel about my light-skinned presence at their father's memorial service?

But I could hardly say no. I knew that Lonnie was Donna's treasure, a boy she'd raised into a man during the hard years of the Depression and World War II, when opportunities for black women ranged between slim and non-existent. After Lonnie's sudden death from a heart attack back in 1995, Donna seemed to fade into herself, her mahogany skin grown darker with loss. One thing that kept her going, she said, was her love for my brother Alex and me. Over the course of 35 years, we'd bonded with her in a way strong as blood. During my weekly phone calls she'd remind me that "I love you just like one of my own," and I'd feel her words surge through the telephone line, connecting Cleveland to Boston to Cleveland in a circuit of something stronger than electricity.

As a child, I hadn't always appreciated the love and discipline Donna dished out with her cooking. A conservative, religious woman, she ruled with an iron hand. One morning when I was in high school, I plopped down at the kitchen table and reached for my Frosted Flakes, keeping conversation to a minimum, so as not to disturb my sleep-induced fog. Donna, never one to mince words, said, "You get in the bathroom and wash your hands before you sit down to eat—and you playin' with yourself all night long." This was something men and boys did—and they damn sure wouldn't be eating at her table until they had gotten themselves right. There was no point in arguing; I meekly did as I was told.

When I was a teenager and my father had his massive heart attack, Donna helped my mother nurse him back to health. Over the years, she had always been there for my family and me. But as she aged, the tables turned a bit. Later, Alex and I (along with her grandchildren) made sure that Donna had what she needed—a new winter coat for Christmas, or a trip to Boston to see her "grandbabies" (my brother Alex's children).

As I drove down through East Cleveland's Forest Hills neighborhood toward the church, I felt honored to be escorting Donna to the special service for Lonnie and the building fund.

Greater St. John's Missionary Baptist Church is the grand name of a small storefront chapel that stands on Euclid Avenue in East Cleveland. The two yellow-brick buildings would

look unimpressive to a toddler, crouching low on the edges
of Cleveland's East Side ghetto. I entered the sanctuary with
Donna leading the way, her face a mask of determination to see
the service rolled out according to plan. She'd arranged it all,
organized a reception afterward, had recruited friends from far
and wide.

Sitting in one of the front pews, I fidgeted on the orange
velour cushions. Donna was on my left, decked out in one of
her '40s-style feather hats and matching shoes. The hat's gray
feather stretched outward from her head, reaching up toward the
dropped ceiling of the sanctuary. The service began as the elders
welcomed the small congregation.

They were aptly named; the youngest was about 75,
with gray hair and a deep voice that echoed in the small room.
Being a Baptist church, folks didn't just sit around and quietly
murmur their prayers, as I soon discovered. This particular
congregation fervently sang a hymn called "What a Fellowship,"
with the chorus of "What a fellowship, what a fellowship, what
a fellowship we have in Jesus" in a call and response pattern, at
various points in the service.

The minister, a distinguished-looking man with cocoa-
colored skin and a gray natural, called the congregation to prayer
in a rich, melodious voice. "We trust you Lord, we thank you

Lord." There were about 50 people in the chapel, most elderly, all various shades of tan and brown. And one pinkish-colored gay Jewish man, trying to keep a low profile. It wasn't easy.

Donna's grandchildren were there, too, all grown and ranging in age from 35 to 50. I chatted with them before the service, hoping they'd be all right with my little speech. Sitting next to Donna, I was praying for divine inspiration—though I doubted God's existence at the time—when I heard the minister call out in his musical voice—"And we are blessed today with the presence of Donna's other son, who has come all the way from Boston, just to be here for Mother Donna." My face turned hot; I hadn't expected such a buildup. Donna often told me that Alex and I were her "other sons" but I didn't know she'd shared that tidbit with the minister.

I mumbled, "speak from the heart" to myself as I made my way to the pulpit and looked out on a sea of strange faces. Two minutes felt like twenty as I told the congregation of the love I felt for their "Mother Donna." Tapping into a confidence that surprised me, I said that though I didn't know Lonnie well, I did know he was a source of pride for my godmother, and that "the apple didn't fall far from the tree."

I stumbled and quavered a few times, and finally floated back to my pew with a relieved sigh. Sitting down, breathing again, and flanked by Donna and Larry — Lonnie's son—I felt the warm embrace of family enfold me in that storefront Baptist church.

Then the minister threw open the floor for other "testimonies" and I waited for Lonnie's children to get up and share. It didn't happen. There was a long silence instead, while I muttered epithets under my breath, cursing myself for being the only speaker. Just as I was about to crawl under my pew, Lonnie's cousin Sandra called out to testify.

"Jesus is in charge of my life," she said, and a chorus of "amens" bubbled up from the congregation. "I want to praise the Lord and thank God for our brother Lonnie's life, and to remember his spirit." Heads nodded. Donna smiled and the service rolled on. The Elders shared, a few more hymns ensued, and after several more calls of "Praise Jesus!" it appeared the program was about to end.

Unfortunately, the minister decided to throw in a short sermon, since he had a captive audience. The theme of the sermon was, "The end of the world is coming, so y'all better get right with Jesus." I started to sweat again, since my people had never been "right with Jesus." I'd never even visited a Baptist church before. But I respected the minister for his sincerity and faith.

I really started to tremble when the minister launched into those "abominations" that warn us of an impending judgment day. "The end of the world is near," he said, and my ears pricked up. "There are abominations takin' place in the land!" the minister shouted, his face clouding over with anger. Abomination number one was, "Men are laying with men."

After hearing that, I didn't pay much attention to numbers two and three. Instead, I reminded myself I was surrounded by family, and my ordeal was almost over.

The service rolled to a rollicking conclusion with another call to Jesus and we adjourned to the 'reception hall' for a modest gathering. Donna's friends and family brought out bowls of punch, cookies, macaroni and tuna salad. I met assorted friends and relatives, her 65-year-old goddaughter, and various great and great-great grandchildren. Everyone was gracious; many began by saying, "I've heard so much about you." I looked around the simple room with its concrete floor and folding chairs and thought of all the fancy churches and synagogues I'd seen in my lifetime. Even without the decorations I was used to, this room contained more love than most.

*

Whenever I go back to Cleveland, I stop by Donna's house. We go to lunch and talk about old times. If the weather is fine and the season is right, I take her to an Indians baseball game. Saying Donna is an Indians fan is akin to saying the Pope has a mild interest in religion. Over the years, as my family connections have waned due to death and my own apathy, my devotion to Donna has deepened. A few years ago, I called to tell her I was planning to visit Cleveland in August.

"That's wonderful!" she crowed. "I'm having another service for Lonnie. You can take me." I gulped, feeling like I had given my all back in '97.

"Well you know I'll be there," I said, mustering my enthusiasm.

And I was. I came, I saw, and while I didn't conquer and I didn't speak, I did enjoy the moment. Most of Donna's immediate family didn't show; it had been four years since Lonnie's death, and they'd had enough of memorial services. But I was there, sitting next to my godmother in her '40s-style hat and matching shoes. When the congregation rose, I rose. When they prayed, I prayed. "What a fellowship," they sang. What a woman, I thought.

FINDING MY PLACE

The last time I saw him, I was standing in the foyer of his 'white white' house, just outside Fort Lauderdale. My brother Doug looked thinner than usual, his red-brown mustache flecked with gray, his lanky frame curving in on itself. "Ulcers," he said—the doctors had been treating him for back pain—the medicine had triggered internal bleeding, and he'd been rushed to the emergency room. I was relieved to see him walking around, looking like the older brother I remembered, though he felt no closer than a distant cousin.

We'd always had a difficult relationship, one framed by my brother's loss of status as the only son when I arrived on the scene, five years after his birth. Once, when I was a college junior and Doug was in his mid-20s, we crossed paths at our parents' house in suburban Cleveland. Trying to forge a connection, I invited him to come along and visit our cousins, twin high school girls who were almost like sisters to me, but who hadn't seen Doug in years. Driving there, I asked my brother if he thought we might ever be close, and he said,

"I've always resented you, and I don't know why."

I'd grown to resent him, too. It seemed during our childhoods that my very presence was an insult, a target for his rage, which careened between our parents and me. As we drove to my cousins' house, I flashed back on our moments together, and the way my brother could make me feel, impotent, as he slid into adolescence, and I, five years behind him, remained small and weak. Scenes flickered through my mind: Doug chasing me around the house when my friend Billy and I accidentally woke him up at 10:30 on a Saturday morning; laughing as I threw a baseball to our father in the backyard, calling me a "wuss and a fem"; snickering that I was a "big girl" at the dinner table.

Years passed, and soon after our short reunion in Cleveland, Doug moved to Florida. He got married, and started a family, becoming, with a small assist from our father and a lot of hard work, a successful businessman. I began teaching deaf children back in Ohio, lived alone, and finally, in the mid-1980s, came out as a gay man. Our contact waned and sputtered until we spoke long-distance once or twice a year—short, stilted conversations that lasted a few minutes and felt like hours.

*

My weekend in South Florida was a grand experiment, my first solo trip since I'd slipped into a deep depression in the spring of 1998. Two months later, in July, I was traveling again. Venturing out from the safety net of my best friend's house in Jacksonville, I headed for the neon lights of South Beach.

My route took me through Fort Lauderdale, within shouting distance of Doug and his family. Though I hadn't planned to phone him, after 300 miles of highway, with only the restless chatter of my mind for company and something I couldn't quite name congealed in my abdomen—the loneliness of the past few months, the fear of being hospitalized, the terror of being alone, and my belief that I would always remain so—I felt needy enough to call my brother, only to hear his bass voice on the family answering machine.

My call to Doug was fueled by guilt, and a pinch of curiosity. Guilt because I'd missed my nephew David's Bar Mitzvah—a full-scale event with professional dancers and a 'Dave's Café' nightclub theme. And curiosity, since I wondered if we'd ever talk about anything more substantial than the fate of the Cleveland Indians. So I left a message, giving him the name of the South Beach hotel where I'd be staying for the weekend. Then I drove toward Miami Beach, wondering if he would call.

*

During the week—in June of 1998—when I was supposed to be with my mother, two brothers, and their families at my nephew's Bar Mitzvah, I was attending a psychiatric day program at a local hospital. A week before the big event, I'd called the phone number for inpatient mental health services on the back of my Tufts HMO card. Desperate enough to sign up for a stint in their inpatient unit, I was referred to Partial Hospitalization instead, a 9 to 5 program that ran Monday through Friday. "Partial" was designed for those who could get themselves safely to and from the hospital, and function independently during evenings and weekends. When I found out that I wouldn't be eligible for the inpatient unit, I was both relieved and disappointed. Relieved, because I was afraid they would load me up with drugs like Thorazine and put me in a catatonic state. Disappointed because catatonia looked like a good place to be at that moment.

I'd just begun my first deeply intimate relationship with a man—starting to work out some of my hang-ups around sex and intimacy, trying to breathe when Terry said he "could love me, if I let him in." Under the specter of his AIDS diagnosis and his desire for me, my heart skipped beats, my irritable bowel growled and sputtered. I began to lose weight; even the thought of food made me queasy.

Though Terry's face was weathered and pockmarked from childhood acne and the losses that had shaped his life—childhood abuse at the hands of an uncle, the death of a two-year-old son during his 15-year marriage, divorce—he looked healthy, his body trim and muscular. But he had tried most of the new drug cocktails with limited success. He was on the last regimen available, and his T-cell counts rose and fell unpredictably, a thrill ride I hadn't signed on for. Terry carried the virus within him, and during one of our first times together, the condom broke. A near miss, but enough to scare me—the AIDS and his talk of loving me when I knew I wasn't worth the trouble. Two months later, I ended the relationship.

During the winter and spring after our breakup, I worked as a sign language interpreter, rushing from one freelance job to another. Struggling to decipher the 'accents' of my deaf clients, their unique styles of signing and facial expressions, I had difficulty eating, sleeping, even breathing. My abdomen tensed and my mind raced, a gerbil caged by fears of what might go wrong. I wanted to rest, to freeze my mind, to relax. The low dose of Klonopin I often used "to take the edge off" made me groggy; I was terrified of becoming addicted to the yellow pills, but couldn't find another way to relax.

Though I hadn't seen my nephew, Doug's son, more than a few times, I planned to fly down from Boston to Florida to attend David's rite of passage. I'd even rented a tux for the occasion. But a week before the Bar Mitzvah, I called my mother, explaining that I was in no condition to join the party. She murmured, "That's all right, dear," but I heard her unvoiced sigh, the ache of her disappointment.

*

Two months later, I was treading water instead of inhaling it. "One day at a time," the motto of the Partial Hospitalization staff, became my mantra as I rebuilt my life during those first weeks of independence. Weekly therapy and daily exercise helped me feel more stable, along with a few weeks of vacation. And so I went to Jacksonville, a place both safe and familiar to me.

Tucked into the northeast corner of Florida, far enough away from Doug and his family that I wouldn't have to visit, I spent the first week sleeping, reading and hanging out with Mitchell and his lover, Lee. Mitch and I had been friends for 15 years; he knew of my fears of getting older and being alone, my shyness around men and sex, my periods of depression, and never seemed to care. After all those years, we'd become 'family.'

I sat in Mitch's yard, soaking in the humid heat of a Jacksonville July and planning my upcoming trip to Miami Beach. Looking in that direction—toward Daytona—plumes of black smoke smudged the sky. Huge brushfires had been burning up patches of northern and central Florida, blackening everything in their path. Interstate 95 had been closed for days. So I planned my excursion, wondering how I'd cope with the buffed up, pumped out Versace crowd that swarmed to South Beach like mosquitoes to a bug zapper.

I'd never felt connected to the gay world. Shy, unsure of myself in bed, and one year past forty, I wondered if I'd ever find a man to ease my isolation. But I didn't really expect to find him in South Beach—I just wanted to chill out. Going to South Florida was a monster challenge; if I emerged unscathed, I could survive anything.

*

Driving down the reopened highway, gaining new appreciation for the length of the state, I had plenty of time to think. The smell of burning wood, the air thick and close, reminded me of my own weakness. Six weeks removed from the hospital, I was rebuilding, hopeful and still afraid. After my vacation, I faced a number of tough decisions. I'd given up my career as a sign language interpreter and needed to find another job. I hated living alone and was searching for a sense of community, or at least a gay-friendly roommate. And I was lonely, wanting to make more friends while feeling like I didn't have much to offer.

A handsome man could distract me from the questions bubbling through my mind, the Wicked Witch of the West fiendishly pedaling her bicycle through my central nervous system—snickering that I was a forty-one-year-old man with no career, no boyfriend, and no luck with antidepressants. But despite my shyness, I had managed to have a few 'adventures' on previous vacations that included a little sex and a dollop of intimacy. Visiting strange places gave me courage. If I got rejected by a cute man I'd never see again, did I care?

I didn't want to get my hopes up. My buff body had been left behind somewhere in my mid-30s, when my gym membership expired and my corky brown chest hair staged a full-scale assault on the rest of my body. Still, I could get my fill of eye candy and fantasize in the luxury of my motel room, watching the shadow-play on the walls, the neon shivering as I danced alone on my bed.

I fell into a rhythm at the beach, and days blended one into another. Mornings brought an early breakfast at a '40s-style diner a few blocks off Beach Boulevard; some reading and light shopping led to a sandwich for lunch; afternoons found me floating in the warm blue Atlantic water. A casual dinner, someplace with a terrace, where I could watch the Eurotrash and the glitterati shuffle by, while I fiddled with my tuna salad.

Then on to the evening's activities—walking up and down Beach Boulevard, transfixed by the blue-green, red-black neon, flashing neon, blinking neon—until I drifted north to a new club called Sporters.

That first night I circled the dance floor of the club, smelling the plastic and woody scent of new construction as I searched for an attractive man who might dance with me. I imagined going back to his condo in one of those South Beach high-rises and watching the sunrise together after a night of sex and romance, while knowing that, in my life, such fantasies weren't meant to happen.

The hours dragged on, and my handsome stranger didn't appear. I did meet two young Germans who said hello and smiled at me. Johann, the tall, skinny one, was soft-spoken, thoughtful and kind. Rolf, his shorter, brown-haired sidekick, was quick to leer at the pretty men strutting by, aping their body language and attitude. I wasn't attracted to either one, but I did appreciate their company. It was nice to have a conversation that went beyond "I'll have the eggs, please," or "I'd like the lime-green ones."

Johann, a psychologist, was chaperoning a group of autistic children from Germany to swim with the dolphins in Key Largo. Rolf was along for the ride. They were both determined to make the most of their evenings out.

"I want to check out the gay life here, mahn. You only live once, humm?" said Johann.

I made arrangements to meet my new friends for dinner the next evening. And since they were staying over an hour from the excitement of Miami Beach, I invited them to sack out at my place. So that night we returned to Sporters, danced together, and had a few drinks. By midnight, I was ready to call it a night and prepare for my last day in paradise. My tiny room featured one full-size bed, a patch of carpeted floor space, and a white-tiled bathroom. I planned to sleep alone, while my guests shared a sleeping bag on the floor.

They had other ideas. Johann had warned me that he only had one testicle; he'd survived testicular cancer a few years before. "This life we got, it's not a rehearsal, that's the correct expression, yes?" He smiled and climbed into my bed. Rolf jumped in on the other side. Soon I was sandwiched between two Teutons who were simultaneously doing things to me and to each other. Clearly, they had been intimate before, and each knew what the other wanted.

Johann, his spindly body shaking, mumbled, "Lighten up and enjoy it," as his tongue darted into my ear; he chewed my earlobe, the nape of my neck. Meanwhile, Rolf frantically yanked my penis while Johann sucked his, and I watched it all—as if from above.

Pressure rose in my chest, an aching feeling beneath my rib cage. My genitals felt numb, unresponsive to Rolf's stubby fingers, which confused manual stimulation with the milking of various farm animals. Still, it was probably me—would I ever learn to 'do sex' right? I willed for the whole thing to be over so I could finally get some sleep.

I'd fantasized about a three-way, but mine involved two muscle studs and a large jug of coconut oil. Meanwhile, the Germans were enjoying themselves thoroughly; I was a gatecrasher at my own soiree.

After twenty minutes of heavy breathing and a number of orgasms that shook the room without shaking me, my new friends fell asleep. Rolf snored beside me, one hand resting on my chest. I gingerly extricated myself from his other hand and draped a blanket over the sandy green carpeting. "Every day, my life is getting better and better," I whispered, as Louise Hay and Tony Robbins had instructed, but I didn't believe it, not even for a second.

We woke up the next morning, took showers and went to eat. Then I said goodbye to the Germans—who appeared more rested than I—and returned to my room to pack and head back to Jacksonville.

I hadn't heard from Doug, but at least I'd made a good faith effort to reach him. Looking behind me, I noticed the red message light was flashing. There was Doug's resonant voice on my voicemail.

"Hey Bruce, give me a call—we're around all day today." They'd gone to the Bahamas for the weekend and had just returned home. Quickly, before I could chicken out, I picked up the receiver and dialed my brother's number. I was still feeling shaky—simultaneously missing the Germans' company and relieved there'd be no more three-ways. Breathing deeply, I calmed myself, reached my brother and told him I'd be driving back through Fort Lauderdale around noon.

"Stop on by—it'd be nice to see ya," Doug said. Though I wondered if he was just being polite, I felt compelled to go.

*

I followed his directions and recognized the house I'd last visited at a family gathering a decade earlier, when our father was still alive. I walked into his 'white white' house and my brother greeted me from across his expansive living room, the distance between us divided by a massive beige rug.

As Doug lounged on his leather sectional sofa, he asked,
"How you doin'?" as if he'd just escaped from the joint, his
accent a mix of Cleveland and Hoboken.

"Oh, great," I said, knowing he didn't want to hear the
details of my life any more than I wanted to tell them, separated
as we were, not by my gayness but our mutual distance, our
ongoing disconnection.

I mumbled, fumbling for words, looking for common
ground, a neutral subject. My niece came in—an attractive
11-year-old with long, blonde hair, I'd met once or twice,
years before. She described the highlights of my nephew's 'café-
themed' Bar Mitzvah party, since David was away at camp.
As we looked at the album, my brother commented on each
picture. "Yeah, we all had a great time—the boy was awesome."
I could see a mix of fatherly pride and satisfaction on his face.
Then he talked about his recent illness, and his daughter said,
"But you're feeling better now, right?" For a moment, their roles
reversed; she became the comforting parent, my moody brother
the troubled son. Her ploy seemed to work—my brother smiled
and moved on.

We polished off the album and watched the Bar Mitzvah
video, which gave us all something else to do. Soon two hours
had passed, and it was time for me to leave. I hugged my niece,

who had grown warmer and more talkative during my visit, and hugged my brother, too.

Our physical contact didn't last long—just a seed of intimacy that never took root.

I walked out to my gray Escort and breathed. As I turned the ignition, my brother stood in the doorway with my niece. She leaned into him, taking comfort or giving it, I couldn't tell. I waved once, a quick gesture of good luck, and hurried north.

Soon I'd be flying back to Boston, where I had to find a new apartment, a new job, and a balanced, healthier way of living. My brother and I were light years apart, but for a few moments, I envied him. His wife and children, his house and country club, his fixed routines and attitudes all set his place in the world. I turned my car onto I-95 and drove north toward something new, filled with fear, sadness, and the wonder of the unknown.

LOST IN THE EAST

On weekday nights, when I'm driving home from
work on the outskirts of Boston, I search the radio dial. With
no less fervor than a resident of an Eastern Bloc nation in the
years of the Cold War, I turn to "Radio Free Cleveland" to catch
a snippet of an Indians game, an update on the happenings
of my old hometown, and a few of local talk show host Mike
Trivisonno's opinions on the decline of the Cleveland Indians.
And if my news is jammed by rain, snow or natural disasters
and I can't hear the 50,000-watt, clear-channel signal of 1100
WTAM AM, I fall into a furious funk that may not lift for days.

My need for a dose of Cleveland Indians baseball comes
from years of sacrifice at the altar of the cellar-dwelling teams of
the '60s and '70s, when I was growing up in a city more famous
for a burning river than its world-famous orchestra or museums.
Following the exploits of Gus Gil, Gomer Hodge, and a host
of other "prospects" provided one more source of heartache
in a second-rate city. But I knew that if hell froze over and
the Indians ever won a championship, I could cheer in a lusty
'I-told-you-so' voice among the faithless converts who flock to a
winning team.

I still haven't forgiven Jose Mesa for blowing the seventh game against the Florida Marlins back in the 1997 World Series. Still, the Indians have provided the excitement of good teams and interesting players until recently. Even though their current owner is well on his way to restoring the Tribe to mediocrity, I've made arrangements to come home this summer and take my eighty-eight-year-old godmother, Donna, to a game at the Jake. Donna's love for the Indians is matched only by her religious faith and a weakness for certain fried foods. My childhood memories are stuffed full with images of her leaning over our red plastic AM radio as the Tribe found endless ways of avoiding victory. "Oh, they're so stupid!" she'd yell, referring to a stream of hapless Indians managers from Birdie Tebbetts to Ken Aspromonte to Frank Robinson. The next day, all was forgiven, until the Tribe found another creative way to lose.

But my sense of regional schizophrenia isn't limited to sporting events. Though I've called Massachusetts home for the last 17 years, I've never fully adjusted to the manners and mores of the locals. Bostonians reflect the climate and landscape of New England—cold and rocky. And the East, while politically liberal, can be intolerant as well—think Salem witch trials and the integration of South Boston.

Simple things that soften gray midwestern winters—
nodding hello to a stranger on the street, exchanging greetings
with a clerk at CVS—rarely happen here. Boston etiquette
calls for ignoring strangers and avoiding eye contact at all costs,
(unless one is panhandling, in which case 'locking eyes' is a plus).
And Boston drivers, unlike those in Cleveland, do not use turn
signals or wait patiently at intersections, yielding to pedestrians.
Turn signals give away your intentions and are considered signs
of weakness—traits of midwesterners and other out-of-towners
who are probably lost anyway.

In short, Bostonians have taken 'Rugged Individualism'
to new heights. Folks who migrate here from slower-paced
regions of the nation are faced with an adjustment process. Some
merge into the general culture—they too become tight-assed and
cold-shouldered. Others—gentler souls who are loath to shove
old ladies onto the T—pack up and head for points south or
west. And a few of us remain in limbo—driving like entrants in
the demolition derby, but still hungering for a smile as we walk
around town.

My Cleveland fixation is a source of amusement among
my friends. Why, they wonder, do I stay in the East? Why don't
I jump on the bandwagon and root for Boston teams like the
Patriots—especially when they're doing so well? And finally

they ask, "What's so great about Cleveland?" From time to time I answer the first question. My niece and nephew, whom I love even more than the Indians, live on Boston's North Shore. But the second and third questions remain mysteries to the uninformed. Deep in my gut, I'll always be a Clevelander. I always feel better on those weekday nights when Mike Trivisonno's broad vowels fill the dark space of my car. Even when the Indians lose, I'm still connected to the place where people care—about the Tribe, and about each other.

Life in the Slow Lane

I am a 42-year-old man with a summer job. Over the past few years, I've stepped out of a career-track mindset and tried to create a satisfying life. As I watch my contemporaries racing for the Red Line at Davis Square—as if their very lives depended on reaching those silver cars—I feel a sense of gratitude that I'm not scrambling on the treadmill of the American obsession with work.

Now that I'm back in my old neighborhood after some years away, I've found that my hometown has become trendy and expensive. And though my neighborhood still has a blue-collar feel, the folks next door just bought a Saab. Rents are marching up, condos are crowding in, and I'm swept up in a sea of 'fast trackers.'

It's not that I don't care about being productive or making money. And I do want to contribute to society. Over the years, most of my work has been in education or human services, a code phrase for hard work that pays very little money. One of my least favorite jobs was working in a group home with mentally-ill, deaf adults. One of the 'consumers' whom I'll call Glenda, was a formerly-institutionalized woman who was built like a linebacker. Glenda had little ability to speak or use sign language, and became frustrated when her cigarettes ran out, in the same grumpy way that coffee drinkers go into caffeine shock when their drug of choice is withdrawn.

Despite my constant attention, Glenda did occasionally run out of cigs, in which case furniture would start to fly. One time Glenda threw a coffee mug at my ear; I ducked in the nick of time. All that excitement and $9.50 an hour, too. But I've always been drawn to new challenges. A few years before my group home experience, I'd read a Boston Globe article about a sign language interpreter—a woman who combined her loves of sign language and theater to translate English performances into American Sign Language. Since I already knew how to sign from my first career as a teacher of deaf children, and I'd always wanted to act, I had a momentary epiphany. After several years of training, I began translating English into ASL and vice-versa, serving as a human bridge between the worlds of the hearing and the deaf.

While I enjoyed meeting many deaf people and using ASL, I found the actual process of interpreting about as relaxing as a drive through the Big Dig during rush hour—on a Friday. During the past few years, I've struggled with a series of illnesses and become a human pincushion. I've tried acupuncture, chiropractic, massage and various doctors, all to recapture

some peace and balance in my life. So after running around
Boston by car, T and foot, I've concluded that I need to change
my life; I need a low-stress job. I'm apparently not part of the
Massachusetts miracle. I will not have the house, the Beamer
and the cottage on the Cape, but like Ms. Gloria Gaynor, I will
survive.

I am a writer who is writing again after a 20-year
hiatus, a yoga teacher who is starting to stretch once again and
a storyteller who is finally spinning stories. This summer I am
working at a Quaker-run communal house. I answer the phones,
clean the guest rooms and tend the garden.

*

I am a 42-year-old man with a summer job. I don't
have a career path. I am not fielding phone calls from high-tech
companies. But I wear shorts to work. I am living my life. And
sometimes, I let the train pass by. I can wait for the next one.

Judah Leblang

WHAT WOULD HE DO?

I'd reached the age where a baseball cap had become part of my fashion statement—an easy way of covering the yarmulke-sized bald spot that had appeared on my crown like an unwanted dinner guest. Shocked and displeased, I chose Chief Wahoo—the mascot of my beloved Cleveland Indians—over a bottle of Rogaine, and began wearing the hat on a daily basis as I bopped around Boston. (Though I've lived in Massachusetts for the last 11 years, I've never transferred my allegiance to the Red Sox.)

And so in March of 2000, I arrived down in Jacksonville, Florida for spring vacation, a much-needed break from the howling winds and wet snow of a New England winter, which typically lasts until mid-April. Coming to Jacksonville was like going home; over the course of a decade, I've made annual visits to the of house my friend Mitchell and his partner, Lee, a naval administrator (Don't Ask, Don't Tell).

Though I find some aspects of Jacksonville life a bit foreign—bumper stickers that say "Go Jesus, He's number 1," pickup trucks in every color of the rainbow—often with gun racks, women with beehive hairdos that list to one side and threaten small children, large dogs named Bo or Buster and greasy fried foods—I take it all in stride.

When I'm in North Florida, I'm on vacation, and given that condition, I'm prone to walk slowly, talk softly, and ask passersby (just like the locals), "How y'all doin?"

But I didn't know just how well I could blend into the local scenery until three years ago, when I landed at JAX International and quickly realized I'd forgotten my favorite chapeau back home.

On my first full day in town, I headed out Beach Boulevard toward Atlantic Beach and Ponte Vedra, searching for an Odd Lots or Walmart in one of the countless strip malls that line the city's streets like the crowd at a Florida Gators/ Georgia Bulldogs football game. Eventually, I came upon a 'mom and pop' operation—Sandy's Sale-a-Rama or something similar—a linoleum-floored and pink-pastel-walled emporium of everything from toilet paper to lingerie. Unfortunately, it was late in the season, and the only cap I could unearth was in a white painter-style number, with the letters "WWJD" displayed above the brim in bold, black print.

I picked up the cap, popped it onto my head, plunked down two dollars and headed out, protected, into the Florida sun. Arriving back at Mitchell's house a few hours later, I asked him if he knew this local radio station. "Never heard of it," he said. "But those discount stores get merchandise from all over the country. It's probably some low-power station in Georgia or Alabama." It didn't really matter—as long as I could shield my alabaster skin from the power of Mother Nature.

Wearing my new cap constantly, pleased with bagging a bargain, I walked around town. Folks seemed even warmer than usual, and Jacksonville had always seemed to me a singularly friendly place. As I prepared to head back to Boston, I carefully packed up my Florida souvenirs—new shoes from the outlet mall in St. Augustine, a multi-colored T-shirt from the 'gay store' in Riverside—Jacksonville's tiny arts district, and my favorite white hat.

*

Several weeks later, I was walking around my neighborhood in Boston, chatting with my friend Kathleen, who was enrolled in a graduate program at the Harvard Divinity School. "I'm doing a research project on this movement within Christianity that's based on a book written back in the 1890s—it's spawned a huge movement in the country among today's Christians."

"Hmm," I said. I wasn't terribly interested in the antics of fundamentalist Christians, unless they threatened my freedom as a gay Jew.

"It's very interesting. This minister back in Ohio created this ongoing story about five people who decided to live for a year by the credo, 'What would Jesus do?' The minister was trying to boost attendance for his Sunday night sermons, and after a few weeks, he was packing in the crowds."

"Yeah, but that was a hundred years ago."

"The minister wrote a book, the book is back in print, and now it has turned into a whole movement of people asking themselves, 'What would Jesus do?' You see WWJD on billboards, T-shirts, bumper stickers....'"

"Uh...'WWJD,' you said?"

"Yeah." Hmmm. I walked back to my car, where my cap, which had been resting in the back seat, had mysteriously disappeared. I was sad to see it go, though it had obviously served its purpose. For a week, I'd been protected, and passed safely through the land of the moral majority unscathed. It certainly beat wearing a yarmulke.

THE ROAD NOT TAKEN

A.G. Bell School looks the same as I remember it, perched on the edge of Cleveland's East Side, just past East 116th Street. It's a slit-faced, red brick structure with tall, narrow windows that don't open, giving the place a fortress-like feel. The building folds inward, modern and at once, mired in 1971, a silent witness to white flight and the steady march of poverty, joblessness, and loss of hope.

The architect Paul Voinovich, who designed the school in the early '70's, was the father of the soon-to-be mayor and now Senator George Voinovich. The building, with its fluorescent lighting and bright linoleum floors, is no longer half-empty as it was in 1980, when many parents of deaf children sent their youngsters to private schools to avoid the trials and tribulations of the 'city schools.'

Today, I learn later, only some of the school is 'deaf.' Now there are classes for hearing children, too.

Walking upstairs in a waking dream, I weave into the main office. I half expect to see Latoya, the sassy, opinionated young woman who held the place together as a secretary back in the early '80s. Instead, two other black women sit behind the high counter. One is occupied on the phone; the other looks at me with a wary expression and asks if I need some help.

"I have an unusual request," I say, explaining my history as a young teacher in this very school and my desire to look around now, 20 years later.

"I'll have to check with our principal. Just wait there."

"She wants to see you," the woman says a minute later and I am summoned toward a corner office on the other side of the secretary's counter, trying to shake the feeling that I am in trouble, have done something bad or improper.

*

I'd wanted to see Mrs. Newsome, the heavy-set, honey-voiced woman who served as assistant principal years ago, who counseled me patiently during my first nerve-wracking year of teaching. But she's probably long since retired, replaced by this small woman who shakes my hand without enthusiasm, a dead fish against my palm.

I'm a writer, researching a setting for a story, I explain. A writer who used to teach at this very school. A fictional story, I emphasize, about a deaf school. It's true, I am trying to hatch a story, but I don't share my background as an 'op-ed' journalist for a Boston paper, or the fact that I'm taking notes about her, and the few other people who populate this building on a quiet Friday afternoon, when the students have been dismissed early.

"Most of the teachers are in a meeting. But I'll get the technology teacher. He'll escort you around. So you're just looking for impressions, just a feeling?"

"Exactly. The story is about a first-year teacher of the deaf and his struggle to learn the ropes." I don't mention that my main character is gay—like me—or that the 'story' is nothing more than a vague impression in my mind. I don't imagine that she cares, just so long as it's fiction.

I thank her and a middle-aged man with a wide Slavic face and pale complexion comes in. He looks at me, scanning, rewinding files of memory, then smiles and nods in my direction. "Hi Rick," I say, reintroducing myself as Bruce, a name I no longer use, part of my personal history like my memories of this school. The principal smiles, too, for the first time. I realize she hasn't given me her name—doesn't want to end up as a character in my piece.

Rick was a shop teacher—with skinny white legs I remember from the student-staff volleyball game and thick coarse black hair, pasted on his head like a helmet. His hair is still thick, and he's thickened around the waist, too, and sports a modest gut. Walking around the U-shaped second floor, he leads me to my former classroom, where I struggled to teach groups of junior-high-aged deaf children about math and science, replacing a woman who had been at A.G. Bell for 25 or 30 years, who seemed as old as my grandmother.

There are no traces of me or my former students, 'kids' who would be 36 or 38 today. Still, I'd recognize most of them on the street, I'm sure, their bored, formerly-adolescent faces lined by life, but expressive, open, the way deaf people's often are.

We walk into a resource room, stuffed with pictures of smiling kids—mostly brown and black faces. I ask him about white children—half the school's population 20 years ago, and now, Rick says, about 10 of 300. I look for a picture of an absent teacher—one I knew as a green-eyed, sharp-tongued woman of 30, with long, reddish hair and a smile that sparkled in the school's fluorescent light, but can't find one. I wonder how life has touched her—gently marked her face, or scratched and clawed her as experience and time often do.

The moments pass quickly—15 minutes or 30—and I feel the present calling me back, shifting plates of tectonic time, two decades sliding together and breaking apart. Rick doesn't say anyone has died, even Mrs. Cowan, the supervising teacher who retired at the end of my first year and seemed ancient, even then. How lucky we all are.

We shake hands—I've taken up too much of his lunch period. Walking out through the dark, glass doors I inhale and taste a hint of spring in the February air. I think of that sharp-tongued woman and Rick, and others I've almost forgotten, who've taught in this sealed box while I've changed careers, and hometowns, restless as the teenagers I used to teach.

Pulling out of the parking lot, I head east, knowing I was one of a hundred transients passing through, leaving less of an impact on this building than the winter winds, which swirl past the slatted bricks and stingy windows, leaving no impression.

Judah Leblang

The Voices in My Head

Voices in my head: You should be writing more. You should be writing better. If you were writing more, you would be writing better. Most successful writers have an agent. Most successful writers have published books, and have an agent, long before they are 48. I am over the hill, closer to 50 than to 40, closer to old age than to youth. I may not get to old age. I may not have my books published. I will not be discovered, though I hope to get something published before I kick off. I could kick off at any time, but hopefully not before I see the Browns win the Super Bowl or the Indians win the World Series, which would keep me around into the next millennium, given that Cleveland teams do not win, rarely win, almost never win.

Why do I care? I do not live in Cleveland, haven't lived in Ohio since 1986, so maybe, possibly, I should just get over it. I live near Boston, with its winning teams, championship teams, and here I am identifying with a bunch of losers from a Rust Belt city that is shrinking, has been shrinking since the Second World War. Why can't I identify with the city where I live now, a city on the rise, on the move, on the Atlantic Ocean instead of one on a smoky river and a dirty lake?

Genetic coding, DNA, tribal feelings, stubbornness, a bad childhood, sad childhood, moments of pain. Strep throat, measles, mumps, hit by a car, scarred by a fish tank, beaten up, bounced around, my body is a map of accidents and bad decisions that tie me to the place I come from like a lasso, or a square knot, or heavy engineer's duct tape.

My father was an engineer, a Browns fan, a Clevelander born and bred, as was my mother. She was not a sports fan, and my dad followed the Indians only when they won, but I can blame them, them and my family and the Jewish people who bred them for my low self-esteem, my deep sense of place, my midwestern roots that cannot be torn up by sheer force of will but need an excavator a backhoe or some other earth-moving equipment that my nephew could identify at age 4 but which I cannot name.

Name what? Middle-age, I am middle-aged, which is not for pussies, not for sissies. But I am a sissy, in the gay community where getting older is valued slightly less than facial boils. Growing less young, which my younger brother, who is happily married to a woman he met at age 17, says beats the alternative, but sometimes I am not sure, though lately I think so, as I've learned to be happy or at least less sad.

Sad, is not so bad. After years of depression, not the lie in bed and stay home under the covers sleepiness of some, but my own version, the style I learned from my mother, my own flesh and blood, which I took with a new twist, blending her anxiety with my own shame—restless, nervous, can't sit still, I have calmed down some, can breathe some, can see better.

Better. Life is getting better and I'm getting more Buddhist, or 'Judhist,' accepting what is, especially if it's not too bad. I sweat the small stuff a little less, mild perspiration instead of a conniption fit.

Fit. For the day, for the week, for the gym. I should be working out more, my doctor said 4 times a week for 40 minutes but the Stairmaster is a drag, though it does have a TV monitor and 42 channels and I am locked in to cable which I do not have at home because I'd watch too much television, which I can view at the gym and not feel guilty because I am working out.

Working out. Things are working out. The Indians will not make the playoffs, will not win the World Series again this year. This is to be expected, to be accepted, to be borne stoically, not to complain, kvetch, bitch. I want to change teams, change dreams, find a boyfriend.

Boyfriend. I have boy friends, but not the one, a lover, a companion. I have my cat, a Calico named Santosh, whose name means "contentment." She is often content, though not lately, she's not happy with me. I'm away too much, as my father was, and why didn't I call?

I've let her down but she forgives me, sits on my chest and purrs her mechanic purr, a deep rumbling meditative "om" that soothes me and brings me back to this moment in which I am still alive.

EVERYTHING IS RELATIVE

I am in relatively good health, I think, even if I have dry eye,
irritable bowel syndrome, and now a mild case of melanoma.
And I look good, youthful for a man of 49—
Or is that an oxymoron?

I must be a complete moron to believe this,
to want to hold onto youth
when the train has left the station.
When will it sink in that I can't wear Levi's jeans, cargo pants
or bikini briefs any longer?

I am superficial. Where are my deeper values,
my heft and and gravitas?
And now the nurses tell me,
I have superficial malignant melanoma.
Isn't that redundant?
Isn't all melanoma malignant?

These words have too many syllables, too many layers,
like the skin that clothes my body.
I am lost among them, looking for a way out,
waiting for the surgeon to show me an exit strategy.
I wait, pacing in the room where he will examine me and
deliver his prognosis, edict, plan of attack.

This attack will include stainless steel instruments,
local anesthetic,
the opening and closing of my skin,
the removal of invisible wadding—flesh and blood.
"Melanoma is not superficial," I want to tell them.

Mild cancer cannot comfort me.
And then it does—I have the promise of time, more time,
and am reminded of its weight, more precious than gold.

Still, I hear the tick-tick of the station clock,
the flip-flip of the train board where all tracks lead to
oblivion.

Meanwhile, I trace the contours of my form,
curiously two-dimensional like the map of Finland
I created for a sixth grade school project.
Freckles grow and darken, erupt into moles,
tectonic plates shifting underneath my skin.

I wear this map on my body.
The elevations are removed,
inspected for collateral damage.

I am anxious for the knife, the cut of steel,
the rich flow of my blood—
but not too much,
that will rid my body of its sickened cells,
and restore me to relative health.

REMEMBERING DONNA

"I'm bouncing back this way," she'd say, along with, "I'm just so thankful to be in my right mind," and at 89 years old, she clearly was. She could recall, and did, her arrival in Cleveland—booming, bustling, industrial Cleveland back in 1943, her visit to the Moondog Coronation Ball—the first rock 'n' roll concert in the nation, in 1952, and her arrival at my parents' house, to work as a cleaning lady, in 1965.

Occasionally, but not often, a gear would slip, just a tad. A few years ago, sitting at an Indians game at Jacobs Field—a meaningless game against Toronto as the Indians were rebuilding and fans were scattered in the stands, listless, just like in the old days of my youth—Donna referred to "that third baseman, Joe Gordon, who played for us a little while back." I'd heard of old Joe, who had played for the Tribe in the 1950s, almost 50 years before our night at the ballpark. It took awhile for me to convince my godmother that five decades had passed since Joe was patrolling the third base line down at Cleveland Municipal Stadium on the lakefront.

But it didn't really matter; Donna had seen lots of folks—friends, relations and baseball players—come and go, live and die, and she was still here, still enjoying the game and caring enough to get aggravated as the Indians lost, and still in her right mind.

And when she did get down—in body, mind or spirit— she'd be bouncing back this way until she could do for herself and soothe her pride, read the Good Book, cook her greens and watch her stories, like "All My Children," "One Life to Live," and "The Price is Right" with Bob Barker who had to be ninety if he was a day, and read the Cleveland Plain Dealer to see who had died, the TV humming in the background.

The house overheated, shut up tight, because the windows would not or could not be opened. Curtains drawn, sitting in half light in this dark city, where an old person wasn't safe in their own home, and you don't let someone in who you don't know, and some of those you do, should stay out, too— and ain't that a shame.

The phone rings, high-pitched, loud and tinny, the connection fuzzy when she picks up. The phone and the phone line are hanging on, just barely, out-of-date like the post-war furniture, wood and cloth, shined or cleaned to a high sheen, and "Where are you gonna get a divan nowadays or a settee?"

Photographs on the walls, dressers, tables, black and white faded to sepia-gray. Unmoved for years, the faces etched in time, smiling men in uniforms, women in church-going hats and dresses fine, faces dark gray in the old photos, and then bursting into color, new pictures from the 1970s and '80s, grandchildren, great and great-greats, with natural, picked-out 'fros or long, straight hair and bright, white teeth.

And then, on one of the dressers, are photos of my brother and me, at his wedding, and later of my brother's family—wife, son and daughter—strangely pale among the cocoa-colored assembly, fitting in and not, out of place and just right.

Today the house is still full of her things, at least I imagine it so. The pictures, the loved ones, the flotsam and jetsam of a life lived the best she could with the choices that she had, fixed her place in the world, testified to the many she loved and touched, and who repaid her in kind, or tried to.

Even my godmother, with her strong will and her knowledge that things would be and should be just as the Good Book says, could only bounce back for so long. Today, the phone no longer rings, but sits silently, as if waiting to be jarred from a long sleep, a waking that will not come.

Judah Leblang

NECESSARY LOSSES

In March of 2006, at the end of a mild but dreary winter, I lost most of the hearing in my left ear. "Lost" is a strange word—not quite what I'm looking for—as if I'd merely misplaced my ability to hear, like my ski gloves or blue cashmere coat.

I didn't think much about it at the time. It was another gray, late-winter morning, and I rolled out of bed, groggily, and answered the phone. I had to shift the receiver to my right ear to hear the caller; my left felt plugged up, as if I'd been in a plane, as if my ear couldn't pop. Days went by, and then weeks, while I waited for things to return to normal. When they didn't, I finally e-mailed my doctor. He suggested eardrops and nose spray, assuming that my sinuses were simply congested.

In the meantime, I had more pressing issues. I went to the dermatologist to check a lump in my low back. While the lump was nothing serious, the doctor spotted a small mole on my chest, removing a slice, and sending it out for a biopsy. A week later, I discovered I had melanoma, and I forgot all about my hearing problem. Fortunately, the mole was caught early, and after a quick excision, I was declared cancer-free.

In late summer, I finally went to an ear specialist. Over the past six months, I'd found it difficult to understand conversations in a crowded restaurant or bar; I was always a step behind, trying to fill in the missing pieces. Before I saw the ENT (ear, nose and throat) doctor, I was given a hearing test. Sitting in a soundproof, glass booth, I raised my hand in response to a series of beeping tones. There were long periods of silence, periods in which I strained to discern those faint beeps, knowing that despite my best efforts, I couldn't catch them.

Ironically, I'd earned my undergraduate degree, 25+ years before, in deaf education. After graduation, I taught deaf children for eight years, and later, in the mid-late 1990s, worked as a sign language interpreter. I'd seen a thousand hearing aids, but had never paid them much attention; they belonged to some of my students and my hard-of-hearing friends, not to someone like me.

Now, after a quick glance at my audiogram, I knew that something was seriously wrong. The lines, which indicated my degree of loss, fell downward and straight across the lower quadrant of the graph, deep into 'severe' territory. I waited impatiently for the doctor to come in and tell me how he could fix my problem. But the doctor, it turned out, had nothing to offer me.

"Hmm," he said. "This is unusual. You've got a severe loss in one ear, while your other ear is almost normal."

"Do you know what caused it? Is there anything you can do?" I asked, my stomach tightening.

The doctor, loose and unhurried, didn't seem particularly concerned. Nothing disturbed his mellow mood, and his air of disinterest.

"Nope, and not really. I'd just say come back in about a year, and we'll fit you with a hearing aid."

I walked out of his office feeling dizzy, light-headed. Something I'd taken for granted, my ability to hear, was now fundamentally changed. I felt older, flawed, a bit like Rosie, the robot-maid on the 1960s show, The Jetsons, who was always in danger of being replaced by a newer, sleeker model.

I went to a second doctor who was a bit kinder, more sympathetic. He sent me to another audiologist, who fit me with one hearing aid, then another, and now a third. From time to time, I sit in the white fluorescence of her office as she tweaks my aid. I respond to a series of beeps, and now, even in my left ear, I can hear normal conversations.

Still, it takes getting used to. During the day, I turn my 'false ear' on and off, and remove it in the rain, wind or at the gym. As the audiologist, a sweet-voiced, southern blonde, informed me on my last office visit, "Not a day will go by when you don't think about your hearing, for the rest of your life."

I'm enrolled in a club I never wanted to join, the ranks of the hard of hearing. Suddenly I'm reminded of the periodic letters I receive from the AARP, inviting me to enjoy the wonderful 'benefits' of being a member of their fifty-plus club. And then I hold the hearing aid in my hand, its oblong shape like a miniature 3-D map of South America. This tool, about 1/4 the length of my little finger, allows me to have most of what I once had, with a few adjustments.

And that's what getting older is about, it seems to me, from this vantage point in middle age: adjusting to those necessary losses, and making peace with them.

The Price of Silence

A few months ago, I went to an all-day workshop at Northeastern University in Boston. The workshop was offered as part of the university's annual ASL Festival, and focused on storytelling in American Sign Language. As a writer, I've always been interested in stories. I'd spent many years studying sign language; now after a gap of seven years, I was back.

The workshop was taught by a deaf professor from Gallaudet University, and was conducted in ASL, without English 'voicing' or translation. As I watched the beauty of the professor's signs, I was reminded of my deaf uncle, Jerry. Today, from my own perch in middle age, I realize that my connection with deaf people wasn't just a coincidence, but a legacy of my uncle's life, and my own sense of being different.

I've spent half my adult life working in the Deaf Community, as a dorm counselor at the Tennessee School for the Deaf, a teacher of deaf children, and a sign language interpreter. By working with deaf people, I've come to understand the challenges my uncle faced in a less enlightened era.

Gerald (Jerry) Cohen was born in Cleveland, Ohio, in December 1930. By the time he was a year old, my grandparents suspected he was deaf; visits to several doctors confirmed the diagnosis. Because my grandparents wanted a 'normal' son who would be successful in the world, they enrolled my uncle in an oral program for deaf children. For the next 15 years, my uncle underwent intensive training, so that he eventually developed intelligible speech. At the same time, he was isolated from other deaf people, and though he picked up a bit of sign language, he rarely used it. In fact, I never saw my uncle sign.

Eventually, Jerry went to a public high school with no program for deaf children. (His education there was spotty, at best.) He played varsity basketball, went to school dances, and by all accounts, had lots of friends. It seemed that high school was the high point of his life; everything that followed paled by comparison. Still, given the constraints of living in a hearing world, without interpreters, without much connection to other deaf people, Jerry did quite well. He graduated from high school, and with my grandfather's help, found a job as an assistant draftsman, working for a local architect in Cleveland.

And yet, it never seemed like enough for my grandfather. I can remember Papa Ben explaining something to my uncle, a vein in his forehead throbbing in frustration, and saying in a familiar refrain, "How many times have I told you..." as if Jerry were stupid or mildly retarded. (My grandfather had a scruffy moustache, which would have made lip-reading him almost impossible.)

Growing up, I felt a special sense of connection with my uncle. As a gay boy, struggling with feelings I couldn't name, I felt like an outsider. Jerry was an outsider, too. No matter how hard he tried, my uncle couldn't live as a hearing person—his jarring, flat speech marking him as fundamentally different than those around him.

Jerry married a deaf woman and had a hearing daughter. But my uncle, who had been taught that manual language wasn't a 'real language,' refused to sign to his deaf wife. Instead, he used speech and gestures, both with his wife and on his visits to the local deaf club. After high school, my uncle's hearing friends married and moved away, occupied with their own families, and Jerry found himself without close friends, marooned between the hearing and deaf worlds.

Many years later, as I worked in the Deaf Community, I discovered the parallels between the deaf and gay experiences. Ninety percent of deaf children are born into hearing families. Like my uncle, they must find their true community and their language—people who sign, people who view them as whole rather than simply as folks who can't hear—outside of their families and immediate neighborhoods. In a similar vein, I had to search beyond my family and friends to discover a community of gay men in which I finally came out in my late twenties. Fortunately, I've had the time and resources to find a sense of community in my life here in Boston, and to claim my identity as a gay man.

Sitting in the workshop, watching a deaf professor, a linguist, teaching a room full of hearing students in ASL, I wondered how my uncle would react to this scene. Jerry, despite his athletic build and physical grace, had died 30 years ago, of heart disease.

My uncle learned to speak, and yet, ironically, his true voice—using his large, expressive hands to 'sign ASL'—was suppressed. I believe this suppression led to his heart attack and early death. Today, when I see ads for 'straight-acting' gay men, I think of Uncle Jerry, and the price he paid for trying to be something he was not.

When each of us lives authentically—finding our communities, using our voices—we empower others. My uncle's experience has empowered me to use my voice as an 'out' gay man in the broader world. The cost of silence is too high.

My Training Bra

It was Carnival Week in Provincetown, the height of the summer tourist season, an unlikely time for me to show up on the tip of Cape Cod. Still, I had the time—a six-week summer sabbatical—and no one to spend it with. So I signed up for a creative-writing course at the Fine Arts Work Center, on the east end of town. Taking a class would bring me in contact with other people and in my fantasy, might lead to connections with handsome men, fellow artists and writers.

As things turned out, my twelve-person workshop consisted of the instructor (a married straight man), nine women, and one other fellow. That man, with his dark-chocolate skin, white teeth and tight, muscular build, was nice-looking and about my age. My 'gaydar' beeped, and I imagined a liaison between us, until he mentioned his partner of 15 years (who turned out to be white, lean, and equally good-looking).

It became painfully obvious that, if I wanted to meet someone during my sojourn in P'town or just have a nice flirtation, I'd need to venture out into the gay masses that flowed along Commercial Street, the town's main drag. Walking through town, my eyes bugged out at the site of one mouth-watering beauty after another, their buffed pecs and butter-smooth skin on display for all to see. I felt like a human blood clot, an obstruction, unworthy of their notice.

I was invisible—submerged in the sea of middle age. Some of my straight women friends, past forty or fifty themselves, had described their feelings of being invisible, of the strange mix of disappointment and relief they felt when attention from men—hungry, wolfish looks and catcalls— evaporated like a summer shower.

I wasn't looking for a one-night stand. I simply wanted to be seen, to be noticed by one of the many studs strutting by in their tank-tops and cargo shorts. Clearly, my clothes weren't displaying my limited assets to their best effect. After several days in town, I timidly went into a store called Bodybody. I'd been there the previous fall, during a sale, when their prices were adjusted from utterly ridiculous to merely expensive. Most of their clothes were designed for men with biceps like melons and butts like cantaloupes, not for thin, hairy, mildly-fit guys like me. Body-squared's racks were filled with clothing designed to expose one's physique: microscopic swimsuits and sheer mesh T-shirts.

But men are visual animals; I needed to reveal more if I wanted to peel one from the pack. My loose, gray T-shirts weren't doing the trick; the toned body within was invisible to the naked eye. (I needed a man with X-ray vision, or someone willing to—as ABBA sang back in the '70s—"Take a chance on me.") Heading back to the sale rack, I discovered that 50% of $200 was still a lot of money. But I persisted and eventually found a sky-blue tank-top, size medium. A bit snug, a little short, but well-designed to show off what little musculature I had.

A few minutes later, I was back on Commercial. As I walked against the flow of traffic—many of the men were heading over to T-dance at the Boatslip, a local bar—I understood, for the first time, the frustration of teenage girls. Like them, I pulled back my shoulders, straightened my back and thrust out my chest, determined to fill out my version of a training bra. For a moment, or several, I felt pretty good about myself. After all, my chest and flat stomach remained north of the equator, and I still had bladder control.

But my pecs, the ones I'd been developing slowly over the past year at Workout World, barely made an impression against the cotton fabric of my new top. As I scanned the crowd—one man after another, blond-haired, black, brunette, all bronzed and sculpted—I pulled down the tank top, forcing it to fit my body. But there was still a gap at chest height as if it were waiting for me to fully inhabit its form.

I was a 51-year-old man, hearing aid tucked discretely behind my left ear, striving for youth, lusting after men a decade younger. But the only look I gathered was from a dusty, wizened character about my age, leaning against a storefront. Still, he examined me up and down, with a look that might have been lust or simply curiosity. Eventually, the shirt chafed against my dry, sunburned skin. The air cooled, and I changed into a loose-fitting, button-down shirt, which allowed me to walk normally and breathe naturally.

The next week, I was back at the gym, doing the pec-fly and chest press. Next year, when I return to P'town, I hope to finally fill out my new shirt. Until then, I welcome fall, with its cooler weather and less revealing clothes—which leave my flaws and assets to the imagination of the viewer.

Finding My Name

In 1998, during a particularly dark time in my life, I felt an urge—a hidden desire—to change my name. Maybe it was wishful thinking, the idea that changing my identity would alter my history, my present, and my future. Maybe I just wanted to run away from myself, to pursue the linguistic equivalent of a geographic cure.

But changing one's name—a common practice at the yoga center where I lived for a year in the early 1990s, was for the flighty or the spiritually enlightened, and I was neither. Rather, I was a depressed man, no longer young, embarking on the adventure of middle age with enough personal baggage to supply a cross-country expedition.

A name came to me—one I'd heard in childhood, when I sleepily attended Hebrew school and Sunday school classes—a biblical name with all sorts of associations, one of the twelve tribes of Israel—Judah, the lion. I'd known a boy named Judah back in high school, an intense, driven, popular kid with wavy brown hair, piercing green eyes and olive skin, a boy who inspired both my adulation and envy.

Now, the name resurfaced and I tucked it away, wondering if I would ever have the chutzpah and courage to actually take it, to give up the story of Bruce and become a man named Judah. I doubted it.

Around the same time, I attended a gay men's therapy group for men with 'self-esteem issues' around intimacy and dating. Since my sense of self-worth was anchored firmly below sea level, I often felt jabs of jealousy as my group-mates went on to date and meet their significant others. The psychologist who led the group, a large, blunt man named Paul, had a nasty habit of challenging me on my old patterns, my habitual ways of being. Of course, that was his job—and he was very good at it.

"You need to focus on what you have, not fixate on what you don't," he said, his face creased by an all-knowing smile, which I desperately wanted to erase by using something mildly abrasive—like lye. Though I had no proof, I was sure that Paul had a partner, had been in long-term relationships, and didn't sleep alone most nights, as I did.

"Practice being thankful for the good things in your life; build on that."

"Aargh," I said.

Still, he did have a point. I had several close friends, my health, a decent place to live, and time off for vacation. Things—like my life—gradually got better, and slowly my depression began to lift, like the morning fog on Cape Cod. Subtly, so gradually I barely noticed, I began to appreciate what I had.

I'd always wanted to write, to act, to sing. After all, I was a creative guy; I just hadn't found my medium, or developed the ability to sit still. But shortly after I tucked away my new name, I began to write. Pieces poured out of me, short vignettes that came from all the years I'd sat on the sidelines, jealously watching other men have all the fun. And finally, early in 2000, I changed my name, starting with my voicemail message, announcing myself to friends as Judah, and then finally facing brother Alex, who said at the time:

"You can call yourself anything you want to, but I'm never using it."

Still I persevered, and 18 months later, he actually called me Judah. Soon after, in the summer of 2001, I returned to Cleveland, my hometown, to attend a writers' conference. At the seminar, we were divided into groups of 10 to share and discuss our work, and in my group, there was a man named Harry, a few years older than I, distinguished by the yarmulke he wore on a daily basis.

One day, toward the end of the week, Harry told me that his middle name was Judah, and that he preferred it over his Americanized first name.

"Do you know what your name means?" he asked me, and I realized, that though I knew the stories of Joseph and his brothers, the twelve tribes of Israel, and Judah Macabee, the hero of Hanukkah, I didn't know the literal meaning of my name.

"It means gratitude or thankfulness," he said, and I nodded, too stunned to speak.

*

Sometimes, when I slow down enough to listen, I tune into a small, still voice, one that operates on a frequency far removed from the soap operas that usually clog my brain. This voice, which has no sound, tells me things that my conscious mind doesn't know.

*

I haven't mastered the art of gratitude. But I am thankful for the gift of this name and the fact that, on some level, my name has chosen me.

PERSONAL ACKNOWLEDGEMENTS

This small book is the result of a large amount of help, generosity and wisdom from many wonderful writers and friends. Thanks to the members of my writing group: Deirdre Barrett, Andrew Szanton, Harlow Robinson, Gary Simoneau, Janet Spurr, and Ellie Tonkin. Thanks also to my writing teachers: Judith Beth Cohen, Barbara Kent Lawrence, Peg Melanson, Mary Clare Powell, Alexis Rizzuto, and Prilly Sanville.

I am grateful for the support and encouragement of my friends as I published and broadcast many of these pieces. A special thanks to Robert Smyth for bringing my public radio dreams to fruition. Thanks also to my friends at Arlington Street Church, and Easton Mountain, and to my compatriots from Kripalu Center and Temple Beth Zion. I am fortunate to work with colleagues at the Program Evaluation and Research Group at Lesley University who have supported and encouraged my writing over the past decade.

Special thanks to Peter Sawchuk for creating the cover for this book and being my brother on the path, Mitchell Marcus for always being there, Yani Batteau for being her fabulous self, and to my family.

BIO

Judah Leblang is a Medford, Massachusetts-based writer and storyteller, who grew up in Cleveland, Ohio. His essays and commentaries have been broadcast on National Public Radio stations around the US, and published in various newspapers and magazines in Boston and Cleveland. His column, "Life in the Slow Lane," appears regularly in Bay Windows, a Boston-area weekly newspaper.

www.judahleblang.com

Lake Effect Press
http://lakeeffectpress.com

"*Finding My Place is a rich and striking collection of essays and vignettes. With bravery and great skill, Judah Leblang tells a powerful personal story, about himself and his Jewish family, against a backdrop of the decaying, multi-ethnic city of Cleveland. In witty, original, dialogue-rich scenes in the book's later pages, we see Leblang take full possession of his life, claiming his identity as a Jew, as a gay man and as a writer.*"

Andrew Szanton, author of *Have No Fear* (with Charles Evers)

"We all come from somewhere. Judah Leblang reminds us of this with easy prose that captures the pain, sweet pleasures and poetry of growing up in a time and place that is at once long ago and ever present in our minds and hearts."

Kathryn DeLong, managing editor,
Cleveland Clinic Magazine

"In these winning vignettes, Judah Leblang lets us know in spare, humble prose what it's like to be the perpetual outsider: Cleveland Indians devotee, gay man, aging baby boomer in a youth worshipping culture. Yet there's nothing whiny in these chronicles that take the reader from 1960s Cleveland to present-day Provincetown and Boston. Most emblematic is his mid-life name change to Judah and his discovery that his chosen name means 'gratitude.'"

Robin Hemley, author of *Do-Over*

LaVergne, TN USA
13 November 2009

164114LV00004B/3/P